THE BOOK OF
Caribbean
Cooking

THE BOOK OF
Caribbean Cooking

LESLEY MACKLEY

PHOTOGRAPHED BY
PATRICK McLEAVEY

PUBLISHED BY
SALAMANDER BOOKS LIMITED
LONDON

Published by Salamander Books Limited
8 Blenheim Court, Brewery Road, London N7 9NT

9 8 7 6 5 4 3 2 1

© Salamander Books Ltd., 2000

A member of the Chrysalis Group plc

ISBN 184065 0613

All correspondence concerning the content of this book
should be addressed to Salamander Books Ltd.

Notice: The information contained in this book is true and
complete to the best of our knowledge. All recommendations
are made without any guarantee on the part of the author or
the publisher. The author and publisher disclaim all liability
in connection with the use of this information.

Project managed by: Charlotte Davies
Editors: Hilaire Walden and Madeline Weston
Designer: Mark Holt
Photographer: Patrick McLeavey
Photographer's Assistant: Andi Barker
Home Economist: Alison Austin
Filmset by: SX Composing Ltd, England
Reproduction: Studio Tec, England
Printed in Spain

Notes
All spoon measurements are level
1 teaspoon = 5ml spoon
1 tablespoon = 15ml spoon

CONTENTS

FOREWORD

The cooking of the Caribbean is a happy blend of different styles that have developed from the varied culinary traditions of the many nationalities who have settled in the islands over the centuries. This ethnic diversity, combined with the region's climate and agriculture, has created a cuisine of vibrant flavours that match the intensity of the tropical sun.

The Caribbean diet is varied and healthy, being based on an abundance of fresh fruit and vegetables and plentiful supplies of fish and shellfish. Caribbean cooking is simple, colourful and full of the flavours of aromatic spices, hot pepper sauces, fragrant marinades and fiery spice rubs.

The Caribbean is now a popular holiday destination and more people are discovering the delights of West Indian cuisine. Further inspiration comes from television programmes that encourage cooks to try dishes at home and, luckily, this has never been easier. Tropical fruits and vegetables and exotic fish are becoming readily available in shops and supermarkets.

The Book of Caribbean Cooking contains over 80 recipes, from snacks and appetizers to exotic cocktails. Some dishes are traditional while some are modern variations on traditional themes, reflecting current trends but using Caribbean ingredients and influences. Many of the recipes are suitable for vegetarians. Whether cooking for the family or entertaining friends, the recipes in this book will transport you to a tropical paradise and your cooking will never be the same again.

—— INTRODUCTION ——

In 1492, when Christopher Columbus discovered the islands of the Caribbean, which stretch from Florida to Venezuela, he thought that he had found Paradise. He brought back to Europe news of a bright and colourful land alive with abundant flowers, juicy tropical fruits, the sound of birdsong and the scent of spices.

The cuisine of the 200 islands of the Caribbean is a mixture of so many styles that it is almost impossible to define it.

The original inhabitants of the islands were Amerindians - Arawaks and Caribs. The Arawaks, who were the first arrivals, were skilled farmers. They brought with them maize, chilli peppers, yams, sweet potatoes and cassava, and gathered wild fruit such as guavas and pineapples. The Caribs were natural hunters who lived mainly by fishing and hunting, and eventually eliminated the Arawaks. The early Spanish settlers introduced many fruits and vegetables, such as limes, mangoes, coconut, sugar cane, coffee, ginger, tamarind and rice, and their influence is still seen in much Caribbean cooking today.

In the sixteenth century, African slaves who were brought in to work in the sugar plantations, introduced okra and black-eyed beans, or peas as they are often called, and Indian workers brought curries and chutneys. Together with Chinese settlers and Jewish people from Portugal, these immigrants have all left their mark.

During the seventeenth and eighteenth centuries European nations were establishing New World empires. Constant warfare meant that some islands frequently changed hands and each time the culinary traditions of the previous occupiers were left behind.

Certain basic styles bring together both the diverse ingredients and the cooking methods from Europe, Asia and Africa, but each national group of islands has its own characteristics and individual flavours.

The cooking of the Caribbean is based on abundant tropical fruit and vegetables and large catches of fish and shellfish. Meals tend to be made with recipes handed down through the generations. Most cooks have

their own secret ingredients which make their recipes unique. Soups and stews containing plenty of vegetables, cooked and served in one pot, are favourite dishes and are often served with dumplings. Cooking over an open fire is common, with meat and fish being marinated in hot spice mixtures. Rice is an important food and is served at almost every meal with meat, fish or vegetables.

Goat, pork and chicken are the most frequently eaten meats, although nowadays a certain amount of beef is imported. Pork is widely used and no part of the animal goes to waste. Pigs' heads, tails and trotters, often pickled and dyed bright crimson, are frequently seen in the markets: pickling originated in the days before refrigeration when it was used as a way of preserving meat in the hot climate. Stuffed roast suckling pig is served on special occasions, traditionally accompanied by boiled or roast yams and sweet potatoes.

There is a plentiful supply of fish in the seas around the islands and fish is eaten everywhere. Fishermen bring in crayfish, prawns (shrimp), crabs, flying fish, grouper, red snapper, tuna and kingfish. Mackerel is cheap and very widely used. As with meat, salting was a method of preserving fish before refrigeration, and salt cod is still a national dish.

The range of vegetables is enormous with root vegetables such as yams, cassava and sweet potatoes being great favourites. Vegetables are often stuffed or made into stews or curries. Pumpkin is very popular and is eaten both as a vegetable or incorporated into sweet dishes. Pulses are served as accompaniments, made into soups, added to stews and combined with rice in the traditional dish: rice and peas. West Indian fruits have become more familiar in the West in recent years. Mangoes, fresh coconuts and plantains are all familiar sights in Western shops.

Herbs and spices season most dishes. Meat, chicken and fish are often marinated in a spicy mixture before cooking. As well as adding flavour, marinating also helps to tenderize meat. Chillies are widely used. Whole chillies are sometimes cooked in a

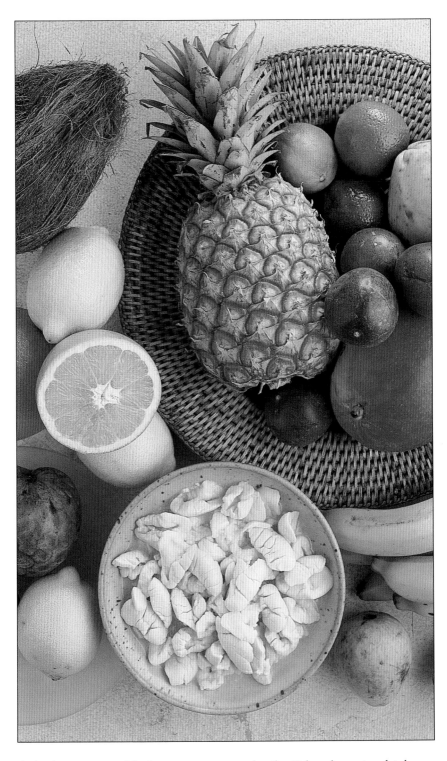

dish then removed before serving. Allspice, cloves and cinnamon are popular spices and thyme and coriander (cilantro) are the most widely used herbs.

Sugar cane is grown in many islands and sugar is cheap throughout the Caribbean; most of the islanders like very sweet desserts and drinks. Rum is produced from sugar cane and is either drunk as it is - dark, white or golden - or forms the basis of punches and cocktails. Other favourite drinks are ginger beer, fresh fruit juices, sweet fruit syrups, sweet coffee and weak tea.

The natural abundance of fresh fruit and vegetables and the plentiful supplies of fish, combined with the varied culinary traditions of the many nationalities who have settled in the islands over the centuries, make Caribbean cooking a fascinating melting pot of flavours from both East and West.

—— CARIBBEAN INGREDIENTS ——

ACKEES
The edible part of the ackee fruit resembles scrambled egg in appearance, and has a delicate flavour; it is available canned. Ackees are an essential ingredient of the popular Jamaican dish, saltfish and ackees.

ALLSPICE
Also known as pimento or Jamaican pepper, allspice is the dried fruit of the pimento tree. The dried berries look like peppercorns and have a flavour of cloves, cinnamon and nutmeg. Allspice is used whole or ground in many dishes.

ARROWROOT
A white starchy powder used for thickening sauces and also used in place of flour in baking.

BREADFRUIT
Breadfruit are large green fruits about 30cm (12in) in diameter. They have a pale yellow flesh similar to a potato. Breadfruit is only edible when cooked and can be used instead of potato, rice or pasta as an accompaniment to any dish. Fresh breadfruit are not widely available, but canned breadfruit are an excellent substitute.

CALLALOO
The leaves of two distinct plants, the taro plant and Chinese spinach, which are used interchangeably, though the taro plant is most widely used. Its tubers are also popular in Island cooking and may be known as coco or dasheen. Callaloo looks like spinach and is used in similar ways. It has given its name to the most famous of Caribbean soups.

CHAYOTE
Also known as cho-cho or chrostophene, chayote is a type of pear-shaped squash that is often covered in prickly hairs, and best when dark green. The firm, delicately flavoured flesh is often sliced and fried in batter. Young chayote shoots are eaten like asparagus. The leaves are eaten as greens and the large tuberous roots are treated like yams.

CHILLI PEPPERS
The use of chillies is widespread in Caribbean cooking. The hot Scotch bonnet is the most popular variety; it is a small, lantern-shaped chilli varying in colour from pale yellow to bright red. Chillies are also available in the form of relishes, crushed and bottled in vinegar, or in the form of hot pepper sauces and chilli powder.

COCONUT
The liquid inside a fresh coconut is known as coconut water or juice, and can be drunk by itself or as a mixer with gin, vodka or rum; it is never used in cooking. Coconut milk is the liquid produced by pressing the flesh of fresh coconuts after the shell, husk and juice have been removed. Available in cans, coconut milk is widely used in Caribbean recipes. Creamed coconut is pure fresh coconut formed into a block and provides a convenient alternative to either fresh or desiccated (unsweetened flaked) coconut. Creamed coconut is either added directly to dishes, or dissolved in water to give a substitute for coconut milk. Cartons of coconut cream, which is smoother and richer than milk or creamed coconut, have recently become available.

CORNMEAL
Also known as polenta or maize meal, cornmeal is yellow maize that has been either coarsely or finely ground. Coarse and fine cornmeal can be used interchangeable, depending upon the texture required. Cornmeal is used in cornbreads, cakes, muffins, dumplings and puddings; it also gives a crisp coating to fried foods.

GUAVAS
The fruit of an evergreen tree, guavas are about 12.5cm (5in) in diameter with pale yellow skins and pink or white flesh that has a gritty texture and is pitted with hundreds of tiny, hard seeds. Guavas may be eaten raw but their flavour improves with cooking. They make excellent jams, jellies and pastes. Guavas are available canned.

GUNGO PEAS
Gungo peas, which are also known as pigeon peas, are popular in West Indian cooking and are used fresh, dried and canned.

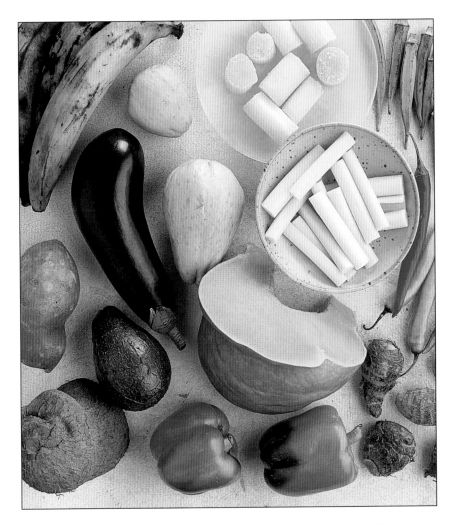

OKRA
Alternative names for okra include bamies, gumbo and ladies' fingers. Green okra pods are prized for the slippery texture that they give to soups and stews.

PAPAYA
Papaya, which can also be called papaw, is the fruit of a woody herbaceous plant. Unripe papaya is hard and green and is used as a vegetable or for relishes and chutneys. Papaya ripens to yellow tinged with orange, with vivid salmon pink flesh surrounding a cluster of grey-black, edible seeds. Ripe papaya is used in both sweet and savoury dishes.

PLANTAIN
A large member of the banana family, plantains must be cooked before being eaten. Plantains are used green and unripe, or when ripened until the skin turns black. They have a mild, squash-like flavour and are widely used in West Indian cooking for both sweet and savoury dishes.

SALT CODFISH
Although fresh fish is readily available, salt codfish is still popular on all the islands. Salt codfish must be thoroughly soaked before cooking. Sometimes other fish are salted.

SWEET POTATOES
The sweet potato is an elongated, edible tuber but is not related to the ordinary potato. Orange-fleshed sweet potatoes have a pinkish-purple skin and a dense texture with a sweet, chestnut flavour. The white-fleshed variety has a milder taste. Sweet potatoes can be baked, fried, steamed or boiled, although boiling can make them rather watery.

YAMS
Yams are edible tubers and come in a wide variety of shapes and sizes, and have white or yellow flesh and a nutty flavour. Yams are cooked in the same ways as potatoes. Yams should not be confused with the yellow-fleshed sweet potato which is sometimes known as the Louisiana yam.

CALLALOO

450g (1lb) callaloo leaves or spinach
25g (1oz/2 tablespoons) butter
1 onion, finely chopped
2 cloves garlic, crushed
115g (4oz) okra, sliced
1 sprig thyme
850ml (30fl oz/3¾ cups) chicken or vegetable stock
400ml (14fl oz) can coconut milk
salt and freshly ground black pepper
225g (8oz) fresh, canned or frozen crabmeat
hot pepper sauce, to taste
finely diced red pepper (capsicum), to garnish

Finely shred the callaloo or spinach leaves.

In a large pan, heat butter, add onion and garlic and cook for 10 minutes until soft and golden. Add okra and thyme and cook, stirring, for 5 minutes. Stir in callaloo or spinach then add stock, coconut milk and seasoning. Bring to the boil, cover and simmer gently for 15 minutes.

Add crabmeat and cook gently for 5 more minutes. Add hot pepper sauce to taste. Ladle into heated soup bowls and garnish with diced red pepper (capsicum).

Serves 6

SUNSHINE SOUP

25g (1oz/2 tablespoons) butter
1 large onion, roughly chopped
1 celery stick, finely chopped
1kg (2lb) pumpkin, peeled, deseeded and cubed
1 small red chilli, deseeded and finely chopped
850ml (30fl oz/3¾ cups) chicken or vegetable stock
400ml (14fl oz) can coconut milk
1 tablespoon lime juice
salt and freshly ground black pepper
¼ teaspoon grated nutmeg
toasted coconut flakes and lime rind, to garnish

In a large saucepan, heat butter, add onion and celery and cook gently for 10 minutes until soft.

Add pumpkin, chilli, stock, coconut milk, lime juice and seasoning and bring to the boil. Cover and simmer gently for 20-30 minutes until pumpkin is soft. Purée soup in a blender or food processor then return to pan.

Reheat soup, if necessary, and stir in nutmeg. Serve in warmed soup bowls, garnished with coconut flakes and lime rind.

Serves 6

Note: Any type of squash, such as butternut, may be used instead of pumpkin.

SWEET POTATO & TOMATO SOUP

1 tablespoon oil
15g (½ oz/1 tablespoon) butter
2 onions, finely chopped
2 sticks celery, thinly sliced
225g (8oz) sweet potatoes, diced
400g (14oz) can chopped tomatoes
grated rind and juice of 1 orange
850ml (30fl oz/3¾ cups) chicken or vegetable stock
½ teaspoon chopped fresh thyme
1 teaspoon chopped fresh oregano
salt and freshly ground black pepper
soured (sour) cream, orange rind and cayenne
   pepper, to garnish

In a saucepan, heat oil and butter. Add onions and celery and cook for 10 minutes.

Add sweet potatoes, tomatoes, orange rind and juice, stock, thyme, oregano and seasoning. Bring to the boil, cover and simmer for 20 minutes until sweet potatoes are soft.

Purée soup, in batches if necessary, in a blender or food processor. Return to pan and heat through. Serve in warmed bowls, garnished with a swirl of soured (sour) cream and sprinkled with orange rind and cayenne pepper.

Serves 6

FISH SOUP

2 tablespoons oil
1 onion, finely chopped
1 green pepper (capsicum), finely chopped
2 cloves garlic, crushed
1kg (2lb) tomatoes, peeled and chopped
2 teaspoons tomato purée (paste)
550ml (20fl oz/2½ cups) fish stock
300ml (10fl oz/1¼ cups) dry white wine
salt and freshly ground black pepper
2 teaspoons arrowroot
450g (1lb) firm white fish, cubed
4 tablespoons chopped fresh parsley
115g (4oz) cooked, peeled prawns (shrimp)

Heat oil in a large pan. Cook onion, green pepper (capsicum) and garlic for 10 minutes.

Add tomatoes, tomato purée (paste), stock, wine and seasoning. Bring to the boil, cover and simmer for 10 minutes. Blend arrowroot with a little water and stir into soup. Add fish and 3 tablespoons of the parsley and cook gently for 5 minutes until fish is just cooked but not breaking up.

Add prawns (shrimp) and cook for 2 minutes longer until heated through. Serve in warmed soup bowls, garnished with the reserved parsley.

Serves 4-6

PLANTAIN CRISPS & AVOCADO DIP

3 ripe plantains, peeled
oil, for deep frying
sea salt
pinch of chilli powder
AVOCADO DIP:
flesh from 2 ripe avocados
2 spring onions (scallions), finely chopped
1 clove garlic, crushed
1 tablespoon lime juice
4 tablespoons mayonnaise
hot pepper sauce, to taste
salt and freshly ground black pepper
paprika, to garnish

Cut off both ends of plantains, and slice as thinly as possible.

Half fill a saucepan or deep-fat fryer with oil and heat to 190C (375F) until a cube of bread browns in 40 seconds. Deep-fry the plantain slices in batches for 2 minutes until crisp and golden. Drain on paper towels. Sprinkle with salt and chilli powder and leave to cool.

To make avocado dip, place avocado flesh in a blender or food processor with spring onions (scallions), garlic, lime juice, mayonnaise, pepper sauce and seasoning and process until well blended. Transfer to a bowl and sprinkle with paprika. Serve with plantain crisps.

Serves 6

— STAMP & GO (FISH FRITTERS) —

115g (4oz/1 cup) self-raising flour
salt
1 egg, beaten
175ml (6fl oz/¾ cup) milk
15g (½ oz/1 tablespoon) butter, melted
225g (8oz) salt cod, soaked overnight
1 tablespoon oil
1 onion, finely chopped
1 fresh red chilli, deseeded and finely chopped
oil, for frying
lemon wedges, to garnish

Sift flour and salt into a bowl. Mix together egg, milk and melted butter and stir into flour. Mix well to a smooth batter; add a little more milk if necessary. Allow to stand.

Meanwhile, drain and rinse salt cod. Place in a large saucepan, cover with cold water and bring to the boil. Reduce heat, cover and simmer for 20 minutes until tender. Drain and cool. Discard skin and any bones and flake flesh. Heat oil in a frying pan (skillet), add onion and cook for 10 minutes until soft. Allow to cool slightly.

Stir the fish, onion and chilli into the batter. Heat about 1cm (½in) oil in a frying pan (skillet). Drop spoonfuls of batter mixture into oil, a few at a time. Fry for about 2 minutes on each side until crisp and golden. Serve with lemon wedges.

Serves 6

VARIATION: Although these little fritters are traditionally made with salt cod, cooked fresh cod may be used instead.

—— PRAWN & POTATO BALLS ——

450g (1lb) potatoes, diced
40g (1½ oz/3 tablespoons) butter
2 egg yolks, beaten
50g (2oz) Cheddar cheese, grated
1 tablespoon chopped fresh coriander (cilantro)
6 spring onions (scallions), finely chopped
450g (1lb) peeled prawns (shrimp), roughly chopped
½ teaspoon hot pepper sauce
salt and freshly ground black pepper
plain (all-purpose) flour, for coating
1 egg, beaten
50g (2oz/½ cup) dry breadcrumbs
oil, for deep frying
LIME MAYONNAISE:
175ml (6fl oz/¾ cup) mayonnaise
1 tablespoon lime juice

Place potatoes in a saucepan, cover with cold salted water and bring to the boil. Simmer, covered, for 15 minutes until tender. Drain and mash with butter, egg yolks and cheese. Leave to cool. Stir in coriander (cilantro), spring onions (scallions), prawns (shrimp), hot pepper sauce, and seasoning. Form into 30 small balls and arrange on a non-stick baking sheet. Chill for 30 minutes. To make lime mayonnaise, mix together mayonnaise and lime juice and set aside.

Roll prawn (shrimp) balls in flour, then in beaten egg, then in breadcrumbs. Half-fill a deep-fat fryer with oil and heat to 190C (375F) until a cube of bread browns in 40 seconds. Deep-fry balls in hot oil in batches for 5 minutes until golden brown. Drain on paper towels and keep warm while cooking remaining balls, then serve immediately with lime mayonnaise.

Makes 30

— AVOCADO & PAPAYA SALAD —

2 small papayas
2 avocados, peeled and sliced lengthwise
DRESSING:
2 tablespoons lime juice
1 teaspoon sugar
70ml (2½fl oz/⅓ cup) olive oil
1 fresh red chilli, deseeded and finely chopped
1 teaspoon Dijon mustard
salt and freshly ground black pepper

Peel papayas and cut in half lengthwise. Remove seeds and reserve. Thinly slice papayas and arrange with avocado slices on 4 individual plates.

To make dressing, put lime juice, sugar, olive oil, chilli, mustard and seasoning in a bowl and whisk together.

Pour dressing over salads and scatter a few of the reserved papaya seeds over, to garnish. Serve immediately.

Serves 4

PLANTAIN, CORN & CHILLI CAKES

225g (8oz) peeled ripe plantain, grated
85g (3oz/½ cup) cornmeal, sifted
1 egg, beaten
50ml (2fl oz/¼ cup) Caribbean beer
1 teaspoon lime juice
4 spring onions (scallions), chopped
2 tablespoons chopped fresh coriander (cilantro)
1 fresh green chilli, deseeded and finely chopped
salt
oil, for frying
sliced spring onions (scallions), to garnish
crème fraîche, to serve

Put plantain, cornmeal, egg, beer, lime juice, spring onions (scallions), coriander (cilantro), chilli and salt into a bowl and mix thoroughly. Leave for 15 minutes.

Heat 5mm (¼in) oil in a frying pan (skillet). Add spoonfuls of mixture and fry, in batches, for 1½ minutes on each side until golden brown. Drain on paper towels and keep warm while frying remaining cakes.

Garnish cakes with spring onions (scallions) and serve immediately with crème fraîche.

Makes 20 small cakes

NOTE: These cakes tend to burn easily, so watch them carefully, and lower heat, if necessary.

ACKEE & SALTFISH

225g (8oz) salt cod, soaked overnight and drained
4 slices bacon
2 tablespoons oil
1 onion, chopped
1 green pepper (capsicum), quartered and sliced
4 spring onions (scallions), sliced
2 green chillies, deseeded and finely chopped
3 tomatoes, peeled and chopped
freshly ground black pepper
2 tablespoons chopped fresh parsley
538g (19oz) can ackees, drained
15g (½oz/1 tablespoon) butter
1 ripe plantain, peeled and sliced lengthwise

Preheat grill (broiler). Put fish in a saucepan, cover with cold water and bring to boil. Cover and simmer for 20 minutes.

Drain fish, and remove skin and bone. Flake flesh and set aside. Grill (broil) bacon until crisp. Drain on paper towels and chop. In a frying pan (skillet), heat oil. Add onion and cook for 5 minutes. Add green pepper (capsicum), spring onions (scallions) and chillies and cook for 5 minutes until soft. Add tomatoes, pepper and parsley and cook for a few minutes until well blended. Add fish, ackees and bacon and stir very gently until heated through.

Heat butter in a frying pan (skillet), add plantain slices and cook for 2-3 minutes on each side. Drain on paper towels. Serve fish and ackees garnished with the fried plantain as a main course with Rice and Peas (see page 61).

Serves 4

——— ESCOVITCH MACKEREL ———

8 fresh mackerel fillets
juice of 1 lime
salt and freshly ground black pepper
2 green peppers (capsicums), sliced
2 onions, thinly sliced
2 carrots, thinly sliced
6 black peppercorns
small piece mace blade
1 bay leaf
1 dried red chilli
salt
5 tablespoons olive oil
6 tablespoons white wine vinegar
seasoned flour, for dusting
pimento-stuffed olives, sliced and lime wedges, to
    garnish

Place fish in shallow, non-metallic dish.
Pour lime juice over and add seasoning.
Leave for 20 minutes. In a saucepan, put
peppers (capsicums), onions, carrots,
peppercorns, mace, bay leaf, chilli, salt and
500ml (18fl oz/2¼ cups) water. Bring to the
boil, cover and simmer for 30 minutes. Add
2 tablespoons of the olive oil, and the
vinegar and simmer for a further 2 minutes.

Pat fish dry with paper towels then dust
with seasoned flour. Heat remaining oil in a
frying pan (skillet) and fry fish fillets gently,
in batches if necessary, for 4-5 minutes on
each side. Transfer to a serving dish. Pour
sauce over fish and leave to cool completely
before serving, garnished with sliced olives
and lime wedges.

Serves 2 as main course, 4 as an appetizer

VARIATION: Firm white fish can replace
the mackerel.

– MUSSELS IN COCONUT SAUCE –

900g (2lb) mussels
1 tablespoon oil
2 shallots, finely chopped
1 clove garlic, crushed
115g (4oz) creamed coconut
115ml (4fl oz/½ cup) dry white wine
85ml (3fl oz/⅓ cup) double (heavy) cream
1 teaspoon sugar
salt and freshly ground black pepper
1 teaspoon fresh thyme leaves
thyme sprigs, to garnish

Scrub mussels and remove their 'beards'. Discard any that are damaged, unusually heavy or remain open when tapped sharply.

In a large saucepan, heat oil. Add shallots and garlic and cook gently for 5 minutes until soft. Crumble in creamed coconut and add wine, cream, sugar, seasoning and thyme. Bring to boil, then reduce heat and simmer gently for 5 minutes.

Add mussels and cook for 5 minutes until they open: discard any that remain closed. Serve in warmed, large soup plates and garnish with thyme sprigs.

Serves 4

CRAB BACKS

50g (2oz/¼ cup) butter
1 onion, finely chopped
4 small, dressed crabs, each weighing about
    350g (12oz)
1 fresh red chilli, deseeded and finely chopped
85g (3oz/1½ cups) fresh white breadcrumbs
2 tablespoons chopped fresh chives
2 tablespoons chopped fresh parsley
2 cloves garlic, crushed
1 tablespoon lemon juice
3 tablespoons dark rum
¼ teaspoon grated nutmeg
salt and freshly ground black pepper
lemon wedges, to garnish

Preheat oven to 180C (350F/Gas 4). In a frying pan (skillet), heat half the butter, add onion and cook for 10 minutes until soft. In a bowl, mix together crabmeat, chilli, 50g (2oz/1 cup) of the breadcrumbs, the chives, parsley, garlic, lemon juice, rum, nutmeg and seasoning.

Spoon mixture into crab shells. Sprinkle remaining breadcrumbs over crab filling and dot with remaining butter. Bake for 25-30 minutes until golden brown. Garnish with lemon wedges and serve with green salad.

Serves 4

NOTE: If fresh dressed crabs are not available, use fresh, frozen or canned crabmeat and bake in scallop shells or ramekins.

SEAFOOD & RICE

2 tablespoons olive oil
1 onion, finely chopped
1 clove garlic, crushed
2 tomatoes, peeled and chopped
generous pinch saffron threads
350g (12oz/2 cups) long grain rice
550ml (20fl oz/2½ cups) chicken stock
1 teaspoon hot pepper sauce
salt and freshly ground black pepper
1 tablespoon chopped fresh parsley
1 tablespoon chopped fresh coriander (cilantro)
225g (8oz) frozen peas
400g (14oz) package frozen seafood mixture, thawed
GARNISH:
prawns (shrimp) in shells
coriander (cilantro) sprigs

In a large pan, heat oil. Add onion and garlic and cook for 10 minutes until soft. Add tomatoes, saffron and rice and cook for 5 minutes, stirring. Stir in stock, hot pepper sauce and seasoning and bring to the boil. Lower the heat, cover and simmer for 15 minutes.

Carefully stir in parsley, coriander (cilantro), peas and seafood. Cook, covered, for 10 minutes until peas and seafood have heated through, the rice is tender and liquid has been absorbed. Add a little water if rice is too dry, or cook a little longer if all the stock has not been absorbed. Garnish with prawns (shrimp) and coriander (cilantro) sprigs.

Serves 4

TUNA BULJOLS

4 spring onions (scallions), coarsely chopped
1 small onion, finely chopped
1 green pepper (capsicum), finely chopped
3 tomatoes, chopped
2 hard-boiled (hard-cooked) eggs, peeled and chopped
1 fresh red chilli, deseeded and finely chopped
6 pitted green olives, coarsely chopped
1 tablespoon capers
2 tablespoons chopped fresh parsley
3 tablespoons olive oil
juice of 1 lime
salt and freshly ground black pepper
400g (14oz) can tuna, drained and coarsely flaked
lettuce leaves OR crackers, to serve

Put spring onions (scallions), onion, green pepper (capsicum), tomatoes, eggs, chilli and olives in a large bowl.

Add capers, parsley, olive oil, lime juice, seasoning and tuna. Carefully stir together. Cover and refrigerate overnight. Serve piled either on lettuce leaves or crackers.

Serves 4

NOTE: Buljols is traditionally made with soaked and cooked salt cod.

CRABCAKES WITH CHILLI SALSA

450g (1lb) fresh, dressed brown and white crabmeat
4 spring onions (scallions), finely chopped
2.5cm (1in) piece fresh root ginger, grated
2 tablespoons chopped fresh coriander (cilantro)
2 tablespoons mayonnaise
1 teaspoon hot pepper sauce
salt and freshly ground black pepper
50-115g (2-4oz/1-2 cups) fresh breadcrumbs
oil, for frying
CHILLI SALSA:
4 tomatoes, peeled and finely diced
2 fresh red chillies, deseeded and finely chopped
1 small red onion, finely chopped
juice of 1 lime
3 tablespoons chopped fresh coriander (cilantro)
salt and sugar

To make chilli salsa, in a bowl, combine tomatoes, chillies, onion, lime juice, coriander (cilantro), and salt and sugar, to taste. Set aside. In a bowl, mix together crabmeat, spring onions (scallions), ginger, coriander (cilantro), mayonnaise, hot pepper sauce and seasoning. Stir in enough breadcrumbs to make a mixture that is firm enough to form patties, but is not too stiff. Chill for 30 minutes.

Form crab mixture into 12 cakes. In a frying pan (skillet), heat a shallow layer of oil and fry crab cakes, in batches if necessary, for 3-4 minutes on each side until browned. Drain on paper towels. Serve with chilled chilli salsa.

Serves 4

NOTE: Fresh crabmeat will have the best flavour, but if it is not available, use frozen or canned crabmeat.

— MARINATED TUNA STEAKS —

4 tuna steaks, 2cm (¾in) thick
MARINADE:
1 small onion, finely chopped
4 spring onions (scallions), finely chopped
2 cloves garlic, crushed
2.5cm (1in) piece fresh root ginger, grated
½ teaspoon hot pepper sauce
salt
CUCUMBER SALAD:
1 cucumber, peeled, deseeded and chopped
1 teaspoon salt
1 clove garlic, crushed
1 tablespoon lime juice
1 small, fresh red chilli, deseeded and finely chopped

To make marinade, in a shallow dish, mix together onion, spring onions (scallions), garlic, ginger, hot pepper sauce, and salt to taste. Place tuna steaks in dish and spoon the marinade over to coat. Cover and refrigerate for 2 hours.

To make cucumber salad, mix cucumber and salt together and place in a colander for 10 minutes. Pat dry with paper towels. In a bowl, mix together cucumber, lime juice, and chilli. Preheat grill (broiler). Grill (broil) tuna for 5-7 minutes on each side and serve with cucumber salad.

Serves 4

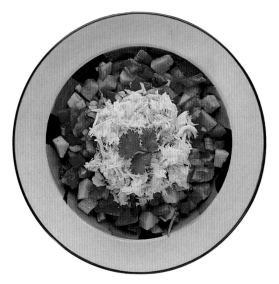

CRAB & PAPAYA SALAD

2 papayas, quartered
4 tomatoes
1 red onion, finely chopped
1 small red pepper (capsicum), finely diced
juice of ½ lemon
salt and freshly ground black pepper
½ red chilli, deseeded and finely diced
2cm (¾in) piece fresh root ginger, finely chopped
1 tablespoon chopped fresh coriander (cilantro)
450g (1lb) white crabmeat
GARNISH:
coriander (cilantro) sprigs
cayenne pepper

Deseed the papaya quarters, peel and cut the flesh into small cubes. Place in a large bowl.

Place tomatoes in a bowl and cover with boiling water. Leave for 30 seconds then place in cold water for 30 seconds. Peel, cut into quarters and remove seeds. Cut into dice and add tomato and onion to the bowl with the papaya. Add pepper (capsicum).

Stir in lemon juice, seasoning, chilli, ginger and coriander (cilantro) and mix gently together. Leave to stand for 1 hour. Arrange papaya salad on 4 individual plates and pile crabmeat on top. Garnish with coriander (cilantro) sprigs and sprinkle with cayenne pepper.

Serves 4

CARIBBEAN SWORDFISH STEAKS

3 tablespoons oil
6 shallots, finely chopped
1 clove garlic, crushed
1 fresh green chilli, deseeded and finely chopped
400g (14oz) can chopped tomatoes
2 bay leaves
¼ teaspoon cayenne pepper
1 teaspoon crushed allspice berries
juice of 2 limes
salt
4 swordfish steaks
1 teaspoon brown sugar
2 teaspoons Angostura bitters

Heat oil in a frying pan (skillet). Add shallots and cook for 10 minutes until soft.

Add crushed garlic and chilli and cook for 2 minutes, then stir in tomatoes, bay leaves, cayenne pepper, allspice, lime juice and salt. Cook gently for 15 minutes.

Add swordfish steaks to pan and baste with tomato sauce. Cover and cook for 10 minutes until steaks are cooked. Transfer swordfish steaks to a warmed dish and keep hot. Stir sugar and Angostura bitters into sauce. Simmer for 2 minutes, remove and discard bay leaves if liked, then serve sauce with fish.

Serves 4

PRAWN KEBABS & MANGO SALSA

1 fresh red chilli, deseeded and finely chopped
½ teaspoon paprika
½ teaspoon ground coriander
1 clove garlic, crushed
juice of ½ lime
2 tablespoons oil
20 large, raw prawns (shrimp) in shells, heads
  removed and deveined
MANGO SALSA:
1 mango, peeled and diced
½ small red onion, finely diced
1 fresh red chilli, deseeded and finely chopped
3 tablespoons chopped fresh coriander (cilantro)
grated rind and juice of 1 lime
salt and freshly ground black pepper

To make salsa, in a bowl mix together
mango, red onion, chilli, coriander
(cilantro), lime rind and juice and salt. Set
aside.

In a bowl, mix together chilli, paprika,
coriander, garlic, lime juice, oil and
seasoning. Place prawns (shrimp) in a dish.
Add spice mixture and mix to coat
thoroughly. Cover and leave in a cool place
for 30 minutes. Preheat grill (broiler).
Thread prawns (shrimp) on to skewers and
grill (broil), basting and turning frequently,
for 6-8 minutes until pink. Serve with
mango salsa.

Serves 4

CHICKEN PELAU

1 onion, roughly chopped
2 cloves garlic
2 celery sticks, roughly chopped
2 tablespoons chopped fresh chives
1 tablespoon fresh thyme leaves
liquid from 1 fresh coconut
½ fresh coconut, chopped
1 Scotch bonnet chilli
2 tablespoons oil
2 tablespoons light soft brown sugar
1.75kg (3¾lb) chicken, cut into 5cm (2in) pieces
450g (16oz) can gungo peas, drained
225g (8oz/1⅓ cups) long-grain rice, washed
325ml (11fl oz/1⅓ cups) chicken stock
salt and freshly ground black pepper
12 pimento-stuffed olives, halved, to garnish

Place onion, garlic, celery, chives and thyme in a blender or food processor with 4 tablespoons water and process to a paste. Transfer to a saucepan. Put coconut liquid and coconut in the blender or food processor and blend until it will coat the back of a spoon. Add water if too thick. Stir into onion mixture with chilli, and cook gently for 15 minutes.

Put oil and sugar in a wide-based, flameproof casserole. Heat gently until sugar begins to caramelize. Add chicken pieces and cook for 20 minutes, turning frequently, until well browned. Stir in coconut mixture, gungo peas, rice and stock. Season and bring to the boil; cover and simmer for 20 minutes until chicken is tender, rice is cooked and liquid has been absorbed. Remove and discard chilli. Garnish with halved pimento-stuffed olives.

Serves 6

—— GUINEA FOWL FRICASSEE ——

2 cloves garlic, crushed
1 teaspoon paprika
1 teaspoon ground ginger
salt and freshly ground black pepper
2 guinea fowl (Cornish game hens), quartered
2 tablespoons oil
1 large onion, coarsely chopped
8 spring onions (scallions)
3 tomatoes, peeled and chopped
1 Scotch bonnet chilli
1 fresh bay leaf
chicken stock, if required
chopped fresh parsley, to garnish

In a bowl, mix together garlic, paprika, ginger and seasoning. Rub over guinea fowl (Cornish game hen) portions and place in a dish. Cover and chill overnight. Scrape off and reserve marinade. Pat guinea fowl (Cornish game hen) portions dry with paper towels. Heat oil in a large, heavy frying pan (skillet) and fry guinea fowl (Cornish game hen) pieces, in batches, until golden all over. Transfer to a casserole. Add onion to frying pan (skillet) and cook for 10 minutes until soft.

Transfer to casserole and add spring onions (scallions), tomatoes, chilli, bay leaf and reserved marinade. Cover and simmer gently for 30-40 minutes until guinea fowl (Cornish game hen) is thoroughly cooked. Add a little chicken stock if necessary, although there should not be a large quantity of liquid. Remove and discard chilli and bay leaf. Serve garnished with chopped parsley.

Serves 4

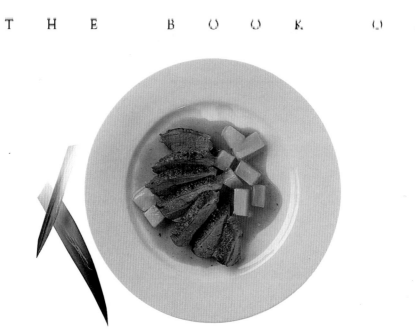

—— DUCK WITH PINEAPPLE ——

4 duck breasts
salt and freshly ground black pepper
150ml (5fl oz/⅔ cup) dark rum
150ml (5fl oz/⅔ cup) unsweetened pineapple juice
1 pineapple
300ml (10fl oz/1¼ cups) chicken stock
2 teaspoons arrowroot

Season duck breasts. Heat a large, heavy-based frying pan (skillet) then place duck breasts, skin side down, in pan. Cook for a few minutes until skin is well browned and crisp. Turn over and brown underside. Pour off any fat.

Pour 6 tablespoons of rum and 6 tablespoons of pineapple juice into pan. Allow to bubble up then cover pan and cook for 20-30 minutes until duck is cooked. Meanwhile, cut top off pineapple and reserve leaves for garnish, if you like. Cut away skin then cut pineapple into quarters lengthwise. Cut out core and discard. Chop pineapple flesh and reserve.

Add remaining rum to frying pan (skillet), scraping any residue from bottom of pan. Pour into a saucepan and add remaining pineapple juice, and the stock. Boil until reduced to 400ml (14fl oz/1¾ cups). Season and stir in chopped pineapple. Mix arrowroot with a little cold water and stir into sauce. Cook, stirring, for a few minutes until slightly thickened. Slice duck breasts and fan out on 4 warmed plates. Garnish with pineapple leaves, if using, and serve with sauce.

Serves 4

CHICKEN WINGS WITH COLESLAW

115ml (4fl oz/½ cup) soy sauce
50ml (2fl oz/¼ cup) tomato ketchup (catsup)
50ml (2fl oz/¼ cup) white wine vinegar
50ml (2fl oz/¼ cup) clear honey
1 clove garlic, crushed
1 teaspoon ground ginger
pinch chilli powder
12 chicken wings
COLESLAW:
115g (4oz) red cabbage, finely shredded
115g (4oz) white cabbage, finely shredded
1 carrot, grated
1 tablespoon chopped fresh parsley
2 teaspoons chopped fresh dill
4 tablespoons olive oil
1 tablespoon soy sauce

Put soy sauce, tomato ketchup (catsup), vinegar, honey, garlic, ginger and chilli powder in an ovenproof dish and mix well. Add chicken wings and turn to coat thoroughly. Cover and chill overnight. To make coleslaw, place red cabbage, white cabbage, carrot, parsley, dill, olive oil and soy sauce in a bowl and mix together. Set aside.

Preheat oven to 180C (350F/Gas 4). Bake dish of chicken wings for 30 minutes, turning after 15 minutes. Preheat grill (broiler) to medium. Place wings on a grill (broiler) pan and reserve marinade. Grill (broil) for 5-10 minutes, turning occasionally and brushing with reserved marinade, until brown and crisp. Serve with coleslaw.

Serves 4

NOTE: These chicken wings are ideal for cooking on a barbecue.

CALYPSO RABBIT

juice of 1 lime
salt and freshly ground black pepper
½ teaspoon chopped fresh thyme
2 cloves garlic, crushed
6 boneless rabbit portions
3 tablespoons oil
2 teaspoons brown sugar
115g (4oz/1 cup) cashew nuts
2 large onions, chopped
115g (4oz) mushrooms, sliced
2.5cm (1in) piece fresh root ginger, grated
50ml (2fl oz/¼ cup) chicken stock
few drops Angostura bitters
2 teaspoons arrowroot
thyme sprigs and lime slices, to garnish

In a dish, mix together lime juice, seasoning, thyme and 1 clove garlic. Add rabbit pieces and turn in marinade to coat thoroughly. Cover and leave in a cool place for 3 hours. In a flameproof casserole, heat half the oil. Add sugar and cook gently until bubbling. Add rabbit and fry, turning until evenly browned. Meanwhile, in a frying pan (skillet), heat remaining oil. Add cashew nuts and cook gently until lightly browned. Remove nuts with a slotted spoon and set aside.

Add onions to pan and cook for 5 minutes. Stir in remaining garlic, the mushrooms and ginger and cook for 5 minutes. Stir in stock and Angostura bitters and pour over rabbit. Stir in half the cashew nuts. Cover casserole and simmer gently for 30-40 minutes until rabbit is cooked through. In a bowl, mix arrowroot with a little water. Stir into rabbit mixture and simmer for 3 minutes. Scatter remaining cashew nuts over and garnish with thyme and lime slices. Serve with rice.

Serves 6

— CARIBBEAN CHICKEN SALAD —

4 chicken breast fillets with skin
salt and freshly ground black pepper
4 teaspoons jerk seasoning
450g (1lb) sweet potatoes, cut into chunks
115ml (4fl oz/½ cup) mayonnaise
2 tablespoons wholegrain mustard
2 tablespoons oil
1 onion, sliced
115g (4oz) button mushrooms
225g (8oz) small spinach leaves
3 tablespoons chopped fresh chives
lime juice, to taste

Preheat grill (broiler). Season chicken with salt and jerk seasoning. Grill (broil) breasts for about 8 minutes on each side until cooked through. Set aside.

Place sweet potatoes in a pan of salted water. Bring to the boil and simmer for 5-8 minutes until tender, but not too soft. Drain and leave to cool. In a bowl, mix together mayonnaise and mustard. Add sweet potatoes and stir together. Set aside.

Heat oil in a large frying pan (skillet). Add onion and cook for 10 minutes until soft and lightly browned. Add mushrooms and cook for 3 minutes. Season and add to sweet potato mixture with spinach and chives. Mix gently and add lime juice to taste. Cut chicken into thick diagonal slices and serve with salad.

Serves 4

MANGO TURKEY

1 clove garlic, crushed
1 teaspoon dried oregano
½ teaspoon ground allspice
salt and freshly ground black pepper
4 turkey steaks
200g (7oz) canned mango slices with their syrup
200g (7oz) can chopped tomatoes
1-2 teaspoons hot pepper sauce
1 tablespoon oil
15g (½ oz/1 tablespoon) butter
1 small mango, peeled and sliced, to garnish

In a dish, mix together garlic, oregano, all-spice and seasoning. Turn turkey steaks in mixture to coat. Cover and leave in a cool place for 1 hour.

Meanwhile, place canned mango slices with their syrup, and the tomatoes in a blender or food processor and blend until smooth. Pour into a saucepan and add hot pepper sauce and seasoning. Bring to the boil, cover and simmer gently for 3 minutes. The sauce should be quite thick, but, if necessary, add a little water.

Heat oil and butter in a large frying pan (skillet) and fry turkey steaks for about 5 minutes on each side until cooked through. Pour mango sauce into pan and simmer for 3 minutes. Meanwhile, preheat grill (broiler). Grill (broil) fresh mango slices until lightly browned. Serve turkey with mango sauce, garnished with grilled (broiled) mango slices. Serve with mashed sweet potatoes.

Serves 4

- QUAIL IN RUM & RAISIN SAUCE -

4 tablespoons dark rum
4 tablespoons raisins
1 tablespoon oil
8 quails
1 onion, sliced
1 clove garlic, sliced
1 teaspoon molasses
150ml (5fl oz/⅔ cup) chicken stock
1 teaspoon hot pepper sauce
salt and freshly ground black pepper
2 teaspoons arrowroot
chopped fresh coriander (cilantro), to garnish

Put rum and raisins in a bowl and leave to soak for 2 hours.

Heat oil in a flameproof casserole. Add quails and cook, turning frequently, until evenly browned. Remove and set aside. Add onion and garlic to casserole and cook for 10 minutes until soft. Strain rum from raisins and put in a ladle or small saucepan. Heat gently then set alight with a taper and pour into casserole.

When flames die down, stir in molasses, stock, hot pepper sauce and seasoning. Return quails to casserole. Cover and cook for 20-30 minutes until cooked through. Remove to a serving dish and keep warm. In a bowl, mix arrowroot with a little water and stir into sauce in casserole. Cook, stirring, for a few minutes until thickened. Pour over quails. Garnish with chopped coriander (cilantro) and serve.

Serves 4

- SUGARED CHICKEN CASSEROLE -

8 chicken thighs
3 tablespoons oil
2 teaspoons caster (superfine) sugar
1 onion, finely chopped
2 sticks celery, chopped
115ml (4fl oz/½ cup) chicken stock
2 large plum tomatoes, deseeded and chopped
225g (8oz) okra
MARINADE:
1 red onion, roughly chopped
2 cloves garlic, roughly chopped
2.5cm (1in) piece fresh root ginger, chopped
1 red chilli, deseeded and roughly chopped
2 tablespoons chopped fresh coriander (cilantro)
1 tablespoon olive oil
juice of ½ lime
salt and freshly ground black pepper

To make marinade, put onion, garlic, ginger, chilli, coriander (cilantro), olive oil, lime juice and seasoning in a blender or food processor and process to a paste. Rub over chicken thighs and place in a dish. Cover and refrigerate overnight. Scrape marinade off chicken and reserve. Dry chicken thighs on paper towels. In a frying pan (skillet), heat oil. Add sugar and cook gently until sugar dissolves. Add chicken and cook, turning frequently, until well browned.

Transfer to a casserole. Add onion and celery to oil in frying pan (skillet) and cook for 10 minutes until soft. Stir chicken stock into pan, scraping up any sediment, then pour over chicken. Bring to the boil then cover and simmer gently for 20 minutes. Add tomatoes and okra and cook for a further 15 minutes. Add 2-3 tablespoons of reserved marinade, according to taste. Season and serve.

Serves 4

— BANANA-STUFFED CHICKEN —

1.75kg (3¾lb) chicken
1 tablespoon clear honey
juice of 1 small orange
115ml (4fl oz/½ cup) chicken stock
4 tablespoons rum
slices of orange, to garnish
STUFFING:
85g (3oz/½ cup) long-grain rice, cooked
3 bananas, mashed
grated rind and juice of 1 orange
¼ teaspoon cayenne pepper
¼ teaspoon freshly grated nutmeg
1 tablespoon rum
salt and freshly ground black pepper

Preheat oven to 180C (350F/Gas 4). To
make stuffing, in a bowl mix together rice,
bananas, orange rind and juice, cayenne
pepper, nutmeg, rum and seasoning. Fill
chicken cavity with stuffing. Season
chicken skin and place in a roasting tin
(pan). In a bowl, mix together honey and
orange juice and pour over chicken. Roast
for 1½ hours, basting every 15 minutes,
until chicken is brown and cooked through.

Transfer chicken to a heated serving dish
and keep warm. Remove any fat from
roasting tin (pan) and add stock and
1 tablespoon rum. Set over a high heat and
cook, stirring and scraping up sediment, for
a few minutes until slightly reduced. Just
before serving, heat remaining rum, pour
over chicken and set alight with a taper.
Garnish chicken with orange slices and
serve with sauce.

Serves 6

—— CARIBBEAN LAMB CURRY ——

800g (1¾lb) trimmed shoulder of lamb, cut into
   2.5cm (1in) cubes
finely grated rind and juice of 1 lime
3 cloves garlic, crushed
3 tablespoons oil
1 large onion, chopped
2 teaspoons medium curry powder
1 teaspoon ground cumin
1 tablespoon hot pepper sauce
2 teaspoons molasses
2 tablespoons tomato purée (paste)
50g (2oz) creamed coconut
salt
1 tablespoon chopped fresh coriander (cilantro)

Place lamb in a bowl with lime rind and juice, and garlic. Mix well, cover and leave in a cool place for 2 hours. In a flameproof casserole, heat oil. Add onion and cook for 10 minutes until soft. Remove and set aside. Drain meat (reserve any marinade) and pat dry with paper towels. Add meat to hot oil, in batches, and fry until well browned. Return onions and browned meat to casserole.

Stir in curry powder and cumin and cook for a further minute. Add hot pepper sauce, molasses, tomato purée (paste) and creamed coconut and cook for a further 5 minutes. Add salt and about 150ml (5fl oz/⅔ cup) water, to just cover meat. Bring to the boil then reduce heat, cover and simmer gently, stirring occasionally, for 1½-2 hours until meat is tender. Stir in coriander (cilantro). Serve with cooked rice or Journey Cakes (see page 74).

Serves 4

JAMAICA PATTIES

1 tablespoon oil
1 red onion, finely chopped
1 clove garlic, crushed
250g (9oz) minced (ground) lamb or beef
1 green chilli, finely chopped
2 large tomatoes, peeled and chopped
1-2 teaspoons medium curry powder
salt and freshly ground black pepper
beaten egg, for glazing
PASTRY:
350g (12oz/3 cups) plain (all-purpose) flour
1 teaspoon ground turmeric
175g (6oz/¾ cup) butter or hard margarine

Heat oil in a frying pan (skillet), add onion and garlic and cook for 10 minutes until soft. Add lamb or beef and stir until browned. Add chilli, tomatoes, curry powder and seasoning. Stir in 115ml (4fl oz/½ cup) water and simmer gently, stirring frequently, for 15-20 minutes until liquid has evaporated. Leave to cool.

To make pastry, sift flour, turmeric and salt into a bowl. Rub in butter or margarine to resemble breadcrumbs. Add about 3 tablespoons water to make a firm dough. Cover and chill for 1 hour. Preheat oven to 200C (400F/Gas 6). Divide pastry into 8 and roll into 18cm (7in) circles; place a spoonful of filling on one half of each. Moisten edges with water, fold pastry over and press together firmly. Place on a baking sheet. Brush with egg and bake for 30 minutes until golden.

Makes 8

JERK PORK

1 tablespoon oil
2 onions, finely chopped
2 fresh red chillies, deseeded and finely chopped
1 clove garlic, crushed
2.5cm (1in) piece fresh root ginger, grated
1 teaspoon dried thyme
1 teaspoon ground allspice
1 teaspoon ground cinnamon
1 teaspoon hot pepper sauce
juice of 1 large orange
grated rind and juice of 1 lime
2 teaspoons brown sugar
salt and freshly ground black pepper
4 pork steaks or chops

In a frying pan (skillet), heat oil. Add onions and cook for 10 minutes until soft. Add chillies, garlic, ginger, thyme, allspice and cinnamon and fry for 2 minutes. Stir in hot pepper sauce, orange juice, lime rind and juice, and sugar. Simmer until mixture forms a dark paste. Season and leave to cool.

Rub paste over pork. Cover and chill overnight. Preheat oven to 190C (375F/Gas 5). Place pork on a rack in a roasting tin (pan) and roast for 30 minutes until cooked through.

Serves 4

STUFFED BAKED PAPAYA

1 green papaya, weighing about 2kg (4½lb)
2 tablespoons oil
1 onion, finely chopped
1 clove garlic, crushed
450g (1lb) lean minced (ground) pork
3 tomatoes, peeled and chopped
1 fresh green chilli, deseeded and finely chopped
¼ teaspoon dried thyme
¼ teaspoon ground allspice
salt and freshly ground black pepper
4 tablespoons grated cheese
1 tablespoon fresh breadcrumbs
lime wedges, to garnish

Preheat oven to 180C (350F/Gas 4). Cut papaya in half lengthwise and remove the seeds (peel the papaya if you prefer). Place papaya halves in a pan of boiling salted water and simmer for 10 minutes. Remove, drain thoroughly and pat dry with paper towels. Place in a baking dish. Meanwhile, in a saucepan, heat oil. Add onion and garlic and cook for 10 minutes until soft. Add pork and stir until browned.

Add tomatoes, chilli, thyme, allspice and seasoning and cook, stirring several times, for 15-20 minutes until thickened. Stir in half the cheese. Fill papaya halves with meat mixture. Mix together breadcrumbs and remaining cheese and sprinkle on top. Bake for 30-40 minutes until browned on top and the papaya is tender. Garnish with lime wedges and serve with tomato sauce if liked.

Serves 6

—PINEAPPLE & GINGER RIBS—

900g (2lb) pork spare ribs
4 tablespoons wine vinegar
MARINADE:
400g (14oz) can pineapple pieces in natural juice
2 tablespoons soy sauce
1 teaspoon hot pepper sauce
5cm (2in) piece fresh root ginger, grated
2 cloves garlic, crushed
2 tablespoons dark brown sugar
grated rind and juice of ½ lime
salt and freshly ground black pepper

Place spare ribs and vinegar in a large saucepan. Cover with water and bring slowly to the boil. Simmer for 15 minutes, then drain and cool.

To make marinade, in a blender or food processor, process pineapple pieces and juice until well blended. Add soy sauce, hot pepper sauce, ginger, garlic, sugar, lime rind and juice, and seasoning. Process to combine. Place ribs in a large roasting tin (pan). Spoon marinade over and leave in a cool place for 2 hours.

Preheat oven to 180C (350F/Gas 4). Cover roasting tin (pan) with foil and bake ribs for 30 minutes. Turn oven up to 200C (400F/Gas 6). Remove foil and bake for a further 30 minutes until the ribs are well browned, sticky and tender.

Serves 4

JAMAICAN PEPPERPOT

2 tablespoons oil
2 onions, chopped
2 cloves garlic, crushed
575g (1¼lb) shin of beef, cut into cubes
550ml (20fl oz/2½ cups) beef stock
250g (9oz) fresh spinach
1 teaspoon dried thyme
2 fresh green chillies, deseeded and chopped
225g (8oz) each sweet potato and pumpkin, cubed
1 green pepper (capsicum), chopped
2 tomatoes, peeled and chopped
salt and 2 teaspoons hot pepper sauce
DUMPLINGS:
225g (8oz/2 cups) plain (all-purpose) flour
1 tablespoon baking powder
25g (1oz/2 tablespoons) butter

In a flameproof casserole, heat oil. Add
onions and garlic and cook for 10 minutes
until soft. Remove and set aside. Add beef
to hot oil and fry in batches, until browned.
Return onions and browned meat to
casserole. Add stock, cover and simmer
gently for 1½ hours. Cook spinach in a little
water then drain thoroughly and process in a
food processor. Add to casserole with thyme,
chillies, sweet potato, pumpkin, green
pepper (capsicum), tomatoes, salt and hot
pepper sauce. Cook for a further 30 minutes
until beef and vegetables are tender.

Meanwhile, make dumplings: sift flour,
baking powder and a little salt into a bowl.
Rub in butter and add enough cold water to
make a dough. Shape into balls about 4cm
(1½in) in diameter and flatten slightly.
Drop into very gently simmering casserole
about 10 minutes before end of cooking
time.

Serves 4-6

PORK & BANANA KEBABS

575g (1¼lb) lean pork, cut into 4cm (1½in) cubes
3 bananas
12 slices streaky bacon
1 red and 1 green pepper (capsicum), cut into 4cm
  (1½in) pieces
1 small pineapple, cubed
MARINADE:
1 teaspoon honey
1 teaspoon soy sauce
2 cloves garlic, crushed
4 tablespoons pineapple juice
1 tablespoon hot pepper sauce

To make marinade, in a bowl, mix together honey, soy sauce, garlic, pineapple juice and hot pepper sauce. Place pork in a dish and pour marinade over. Cover and leave in a cool place for at least 2 hours, turning occasionally. Cut each banana into 4 equal lengths. Roll each piece in a slice of bacon.

Preheat grill (broiler). Thread 6 skewers with alternate pieces of red pepper (capsicum), pork, green pepper (capsicum), pork, pineapple, banana and so on. Place skewers in a foil-lined grill (broiler) pan and cook for 10-15 minutes, turning occasionally and brushing with marinade, until pork is cooked through. Serve with rice.

Serves 6

PIONONOS & PLANTAIN

3 ripe plantains, peeled
2 eggs, beaten
oil, for frying
FILLING:
1 tablespoon oil
1 onion, finely chopped
1 clove garlic, crushed
450g (1lb) lean minced (ground) beef
50g (2oz) ham, minced (ground)
2 tomatoes, peeled and chopped
1 small green pepper (capsicum), finely chopped
1 tablespoon chopped fresh oregano
salt and freshly ground black pepper
juice of ½ lime
1 tablespoon capers, chopped
8 pimento-stuffed olives, chopped

Cut each plantain into 4 slices lengthwise.
In a frying pan (skillet), heat 2 tablespoons
oil. Cook a few plantain slices at a time for
4 minutes, turning once, until browned.
Drain on paper towels. When cool enough to
handle, bend each slice into a circle and
secure with a wooden cocktail stick
(toothpick). Set aside. To make filling, heat
oil in pan. Add onion and garlic and cook for
10 minutes. Add beef and stir until browned.
Add ham, tomatoes, green pepper (capsicum), oregano, seasoning and lime juice.
Cook for 10-15 minutes, stirring frequently
until thick. Stir in capers and olives.

Fill each plantain ring with mixture and
brush beaten egg over plantain rings,
coating all sides. In a deep frying pan
(skillet), heat enough oil to come half way
up plantain rings. Fry in batches for 2-3
minutes each side, turning gently, until
golden brown. Drain on paper towels before
serving with Rice and Peas (see page 61).

Serves 6

CARIBBEAN MEATBALLS

3 tablespoons oil
1 onion, finely chopped
450g (1lb) lean minced (ground) pork
50g (2oz/1 cup) fresh breadcrumbs
1 egg, beaten
¼-½ teaspoon chilli powder
1 teaspoon ground coriander
salt and freshly ground black pepper
TOMATO SAUCE:
2 tablespoons oil
1 onion, finely chopped
1 clove garlic, crushed
3 celery sticks, chopped
400g (14oz) can chopped tomatoes
1 teaspoon molasses
chopped fresh coriander (cilantro), to garnish

In a saucepan, heat half the oil. Add onion and cook for 10 minutes until soft. Set aside to cool. In a bowl, mix together onion, pork, breadcrumbs, egg, chilli powder, coriander and seasoning until thoroughly combined. Divide mixture into 24 and form into balls. Set aside.

To make sauce, in a saucepan heat oil. Add onion, garlic and celery and cook for 10 minutes until soft. Add tomatoes, molasses and seasoning. Bring to the boil, cover and simmer for 15 minutes. Meanwhile, in a frying pan (skillet), heat remaining oil. Fry meatballs, in batches if necessary, until brown on all sides. With a slotted spoon, transfer meatballs to the sauce. Simmer gently for 20 minutes. Serve garnished with chopped coriander (cilantro).

Serves 4-6

PICADILLO

2 tablespoons oil
2 onions, finely chopped
2 cloves garlic, crushed
1 green pepper (capsicum), chopped
1 red pepper (capsicum), chopped
1 green chilli, finely chopped
700g (1½lb) minced (ground) beef
450g (1lb) tomatoes, peeled and chopped
½ teaspoon cumin seeds
2 teaspoons dried oregano
2 tablespoons raisins
salt and freshly ground black pepper
40g (1½oz) pimento-stuffed olives, sliced
1 tablespoon capers
rings of green and red peppers (capsicums), to
    garnish

In a large, heavy-based frying pan (skillet),
heat oil. Add onions, garlic, green and red
peppers (capsicums) and chilli and cook for
10 minutes until soft Add beef and cook,
stirring, until browned.

Add tomatoes, cumin, oregano, raisins and
seasoning and simmer gently, uncovered,
stirring frequently, for 20 minutes until
meat is cooked and mixture is well blended.
Add olives and capers and cook for
5 minutes. Transfer to a heated serving dish
and garnish with pepper (capsicum) rings.

Serves 6

Note: Picadillo is traditionally served,
topped with a fried egg and fried plantains,
with black beans and rice.

— FRIED PLANTAIN & SPINACH —

1 large plantain
15g (½oz/1 tablespoon) butter
1 tablespoon oil
4 spring onions (scallions), roughly chopped
225g (8oz) small spinach leaves
freshly grated nutmeg, to taste
salt and freshly ground black pepper
fresh red chilli slices, to garnish

Cut ends off plantain. Slit skin lengthwise in several places, then peel off the strips of skin. Cut plantain into cubes.

In a frying pan (skillet), heat butter and oil. Add plantain cubes and fry for 3-4 minutes, turning frequently, until golden brown and cooked. Add spring onions (scallions) and cook for 1 more minute.

Add spinach and cook for 1 minute until just wilted. Sprinkle with nutmeg and seasoning. Garnish with slices of red chilli.

Serves 4

——— GREEN BANANA CURRY ———

5 green bananas
2 tablespoons oil
1 onion, finely sliced
1 tablespoon curry paste
400ml (14fl oz) can coconut milk
salt and freshly ground black pepper
GARNISH:
chopped fresh coriander (cilantro)
lime wedges

Slice skin off bananas and cut flesh into
2.5cm (1in) slices. Heat oil in a deep frying
pan (skillet) and fry banana slices, in
batches, until lightly browned on each side.
Set aside. Add onion to pan and cook for
10 minutes until soft. Return banana slices
to pan and stir in curry paste.

Add half the coconut milk and stir well.
Cook for 10 minutes over a low heat then
add seasoning. Pour in remaining coconut
milk and simmer until mixture thickens and
the bananas break down a little. Garnish
with coriander (cilantro) and lime wedges
and serve immediately.

Serves 4

OKRA & TOMATOES

450g (1lb) fresh young okra
3 tablespoons olive oil
1 small onion, chopped
1 stick celery, chopped
1 red chilli, finely chopped
1 clove garlic, crushed
450g (1lb) tomatoes, peeled and chopped
1 tablespoon lime juice
salt and freshly ground black pepper
1 teaspoon sugar
chopped fresh parsley, to garnish

Cut stalks off okra, taking care not to pierce pods. In a large frying pan (skillet), heat oil. Add onion and celery and cook gently for 10 minutes until soft. Add okra, chilli and garlic and turn carefully in the oil. Cook for 5 minutes.

Add tomatoes, lime juice, seasoning and sugar. Cover and simmer gently for 10 minutes. Remove the lid and cook for a further 10 minutes until okra are tender and the sauce reduced. If sauce becomes too dry, add a little water. Serve hot or cold, garnished with chopped parsley.

Serves 4-6

—— CURRIED POTATO ROTI ——

250g (9oz/2¼ cups) plain (all-purpose) flour
2 teaspoons baking powder
oil, for brushing
yogurt, to serve
POTATO CURRY FILLING:
2 tablespoons oil
1 small onion, finely chopped
1 clove garlic, thinly sliced
1 tablespoon curry powder
450g (1lb) potatoes, cut into small cubes
salt

To make filling, in a saucepan, heat oil. Add onion and garlic and cook gently for 10 minutes until soft. Add curry powder and stir for 2-3 minutes. Add potatoes, salt and 150ml (5fl oz/⅔ cup) water. Cover and simmer gently for 10-15 minutes until tender and quite dry. Set aside. Sift flour, baking powder and salt into a bowl. Stir in enough water to make a stiff dough. Knead until smooth. Divide dough into 8 and roll each piece into a 10cm (4in) circle. Brush with oil and roll into balls again. Cover and leave for 20 minutes.

Roll out dough balls into 15cm (6in) circles. Place a spoonful of filling in centre of each circle. Fold edges over to enclose filling. Roll lightly on each side with a rolling pin. Brush with oil. Heat a heavy frying pan (skillet) and cook roti for 3 minutes on each side or until browned. Serve with yogurt.

Serves 4

CHICKPEA CAKES & CHILLI RELISH

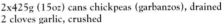

2x425g (15oz) cans chickpeas (garbanzos), drained
2 cloves garlic, crushed
1 bunch spring onions (scallions), chopped
2 teaspoons ground cumin
2 tablespoons chopped fresh coriander (cilantro)
1 small egg, beaten
2 tablespoons plain (all-purpose) flour
salt and freshly ground black pepper
seasoned flour, for shaping
oil, for shallow frying
CHILLI RELISH:
4 tomatoes, peeled and diced
2 fresh red chillies, deseeded and finely chopped
1 small red onion, finely chopped
juice of 1 lime
3 tablespoons chopped fresh coriander (cilantro)

In a blender or food processor, process chickpeas (garbanzos) until smooth. Add garlic, spring onions (scallions) and cumin. Process again until well combined. Spoon into a bowl and stir in fresh coriander (cilantro), egg, flour and seasoning. Mix well; if very soft, add a little more flour. Chill for about 30 minutes to firm up.

Meanwhile, make chilli relish. In a bowl, mix together all ingredients and salt. Set aside. With floured hands, shape chickpea (garbanzo) mixture into 12 cakes. In a frying pan (skillet), heat oil and fry cakes, in batches if necessary, for 2-3 minutes on each side, until crisp and golden. Drain on paper towels and serve with chilli relish.

Serves 4

—— CARIBBEAN RATATOUILLE ——

2 tablespoons oil
1 large onion, thinly sliced
2 cloves garlic, crushed
1 red chilli, deseeded and finely chopped
1 aubergine (eggplant), peeled and cut into 2.5cm
 (1in) cubes
1 red pepper (capsicum), cut into cubes
1 green pepper (capsicum), cut into cubes
115g (4oz) okra, sliced
1 chayote, peeled, deseeded and chopped
450g (1lb) tomatoes, peeled and roughly chopped
1 teaspoon sugar
1 teaspoon dried thyme
2 teaspoons chopped fresh basil
salt and freshly ground black pepper
fresh basil leaves, to garnish

Heat oil in a flameproof casserole. Add onion and cook for 10 minutes until soft. Stir in garlic and chilli and cook for 2 more minutes. Stir in aubergine (eggplant), red and green peppers (capsicums), okra, chayote, tomatoes, sugar, thyme, basil and seasoning.

Cover and cook gently for 20-30 minutes, stirring occasionally, until vegetables are almost cooked. Remove lid and simmer for a few minutes until vegetables are tender and most of the liquid has evaporated. Serve hot or cold, garnished with basil leaves.

Serves 6

VARIATION: The vegetables may be varied according to taste and what is available. Courgettes (zucchini) and celery may be used instead of chayote and okra.

──── ROAST SPICED PUMPKIN ────

1 small pumpkin or large butternut squash
1 teaspoon coriander seeds
2 teaspoons allspice berries
2 small dried chillies
1 teaspoon dried thyme
salt
½ teaspoon black peppercorns
1 clove garlic
1 tablespoon oil

Preheat oven to 200C (400F/Gas 6). Cut pumpkin or squash in half and remove seeds. Do not peel. Cut each half lengthwise into wedges about 2.5cm (1in) thick. In a mortar and pestle or spice grinder, grind together coriander seeds, allspice berries, chillies, thyme, salt, peppercorns and garlic, to make a coarse powder.

Place pumpkin or squash slices in a roasting tin (pan). Add spices and oil and toss pumpkin or squash in mixture to coat thoroughly. Roast for 30 minutes until pumpkin or squash is tender and lightly browned.

Serves 6

BEAN SALAD

225g (8oz/1¼ cups) red kidney beans, soaked
  overnight
sprig fresh thyme
4 sticks celery, chopped
1 green pepper (capsicum), chopped
1 small red onion, finely chopped
salad leaves, to serve
celery leaves, to garnish
DRESSING:
4 tablespoons olive oil
1 tablespoon lime juice
½-1 teaspoon hot pepper sauce
1 teaspoon sugar
1 tablespoon chopped fresh coriander (cilantro)
salt

Drain beans and put in a large saucepan
with thyme sprig and plenty of cold water.
Bring to the boil and boil vigorously for
10 minutes. Reduce heat, cover pan and
simmer for 45-60 minutes until beans are
tender. Drain beans and remove and discard
thyme.

To make dressing, in a bowl whisk together
olive oil, lime juice, hot pepper sauce, sugar,
coriander (cilantro) and salt. Pour over
warm beans, mix together thoroughly and
leave to cool. Gently stir in celery, green
pepper (capsicum) and onion. Arrange salad
leaves in a serving bowl and pile beans on
top. Garnish with celery leaves.

Serves 4

YAM SALAD

700g (1½lb) yam
2 dill pickles, sliced
2 hard-boiled (hard-cooked) eggs, quartered
8 cherry tomatoes, halved
¼ cucumber, peeled and diced
4 spring onions (scallions), sliced
1 fresh red chilli, deseeded and finely chopped
1 tablespoon chopped fresh chives
DRESSING:
150ml (5fl oz/⅔ cup) mayonnaise
4 tablespoons crème fraîche
2 tablespoons lime juice
salt and freshly ground black pepper

To make dressing, in a bowl, mix together mayonnaise, crème fraîche, lime juice and seasoning. Set aside. Place unpeeled yam in a saucepan. Cover with cold water, add salt and bring to the boil. Cover and simmer for 25-30 minutes until tender. Drain. When cool enough to handle, peel yam and cut into cubes. Place yam cubes in a large bowl and pour dressing over. Mix well to coat and leave to cool.

Carefully stir in dill pickles, eggs, cherry tomatoes, cucumber, spring onions (scallions), chilli, chives and seasoning. Transfer to a serving bowl, cover and chill for 1 hour.

Serves 6

RICE & PEAS

350g (12oz/2 cups) basmati rice, washed and soaked
 for 1 hour
450ml (16fl oz) can coconut milk
1 sprig fresh thyme
1 Scotch bonnet chilli
salt and freshly ground black pepper
1 tablespoon oil
4 spring onions (scallions), sliced
1 clove garlic, crushed
400g (14oz) can gungo peas, drained and rinsed

Drain rice and put in a saucepan with
coconut milk, thyme, chilli and salt. Bring
to the boil and stir once. Lower heat so
liquid simmers gently, cover with a tightly
fitting lid and cook for 10-12 minutes until
rice is tender and liquid is absorbed.

Meanwhile, heat oil in a large pan. Add
spring onions (scallions) and garlic and
cook for 2-3 minutes. Remove thyme and
chilli from rice and discard. Carefully stir
spring onion (scallion) mixture, gungo peas
and freshly ground black pepper into rice
and heat through gently.

Serves 6

——— JAMAICAN RICE SALAD ———

225g (8oz/1⅓ cups) long-grain rice
salt and freshly ground black pepper
1 red pepper (capsicum), halved
1 yellow pepper (capsicum), halved
1 fresh green chilli, deseeded and finely chopped
85g (3oz/¾ cup) roasted, salted cashew nuts
flesh of ½ coconut, coarsely grated
50g (2oz/⅓ cup) seedless raisins
grated rind and juice of ½ orange
150ml (5fl oz/⅔ cup) mayonnaise
1 banana, sliced
chopped fresh chives, to garnish

In a pan of boiling salted water, cook rice for 10-15 minutes until tender. Drain then rinse under cold running water. Drain again and set aside. Preheat grill (broiler). Grill (broil) peppers (capsicums), skin side up, and cook until skins have blackened. Place in a plastic bag until cool enough to handle then peel off skins and cut flesh into strips.

In a bowl, stir together rice, peppers (capsicums), chilli, cashew nuts, coconut and raisins. In another bowl, mix orange rind and juice with mayonnaise. Stir mayonnaise into rice mixture then carefully stir in banana. Transfer to a serving dish, scatter with chives and serve immediately.

Serves 6

-VEGETABLE & COCONUT CURRY-

1 butternut squash, peeled, deseeded and cubed
2 sweet potatoes, cubed
2 carrots, cubed
3 tablespoons oil
3 cloves garlic, crushed
1 large onion, chopped
1 fresh red chilli, deseeded and finely chopped
1 teaspoon ground cumin
2 teaspoons medium curry powder
2 teaspoons molasses
2 tablespoons tomato pureé (paste)
50g (2oz) creamed coconut
salt
150ml (5fl oz/⅔ cup) vegetable stock
finely grated rind and juice of 1 lime
1 tablespoon chopped fresh coriander (cilantro)

Place squash, sweet potatoes and carrots in a pan of salted water. Bring to the boil and simmer for 5-8 minutes until barely tender. Drain and set aside. In a flameproof casserole heat oil. Add garlic and onion and cook for 10 minutes until soft. Stir in chilli, cumin and curry powder and cook for a further minute.

Add molasses, tomato pureé (paste), and creamed coconut and cook for 1 minute. Add salt, stock, lime rind and juice and vegetables. Bring to the boil then reduce the heat, cover and simmer gently, stirring occasionally, for 10-15 minutes until vegetables are soft. Stir in coriander (cilantro). Serve with rice.

Serves 4

- PALM HEART & PAPAYA SALAD -

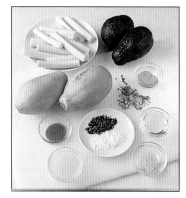

2 ripe papayas
2 firm, ripe avocados
400g (14oz) can palm hearts, drained and sliced
lime rind, to garnish
DRESSING:
juice of 1 lime
1 teaspoon Dijon mustard
1 teaspoon hot pepper sauce
1 clove garlic, crushed
salt and freshly ground black pepper
4 tablespoons olive oil

To make the dressing, in a bowl whisk together lime juice, mustard, hot pepper sauce, garlic, seasoning and olive oil. Set aside. Cut papayas in half and scoop out the seeds. Remove the skin and cut into 8 slices lengthwise.

Peel avocados, cut in half and discard stones (pits). Slice lengthwise. Arrange palm hearts, and avocado and papaya slices on 6 plates and drizzle the dressing over. Garnish with lime rind and serve immediately.

Serves 6

CALLALOO GRATIN

butter, for greasing
1 tablespoon oil
1 large onion, chopped
1 clove garlic, crushed
575g (20oz) can callaloo, drained
100g (3½oz/scant 1 cup) Cheddar cheese, grated
2 eggs, beaten
½ teaspoon freshly grated nutmeg
salt and freshly ground black pepper
2 tablespoons fresh breadcrumbs

Preheat oven to 180C (350F/Gas 4). Butter an ovenproof dish. Heat oil in a frying pan (skillet). Add onion and garlic and cook for 10 minutes until soft. Add callaloo and cook until excess moisture has evaporated. Leave to cool. Set aside 2 tablespoons cheese and place remainder in a bowl with eggs, nutmeg and seasoning. Mix together thoroughly.

Stir cooled callaloo mixture into bowl. Pour into prepared dish. Scatter reserved cheese and the breadcrumbs on top. Bake for 45 minutes until firm and lightly browned.

Serves 4

GRENADAN COO-COO

400ml (14fl oz) can coconut milk
225g (8oz/1¾ cups) coarse cornmeal
oil, for shallow frying and/or brushing
PAPAYA SALSA:
1 papaya
½ small red onion, finely diced
1 fresh chilli, deseeded and finely chopped
3 tablespoons chopped fresh coriander (cilantro)
grated rind and juice of 1 lime
salt and freshly ground black pepper

To make salsa, cut papaya in half and scoop out the seeds. Remove the skin, cut the flesh into small dice and place in a bowl. Add onion, chilli, coriander (cilantro), lime rind and juice and salt. Mix well and set aside. Pour coconut milk into a pan with 450ml (16fl oz/2 cups) water. Add seasoning. Bring to the boil and pour in cornmeal in a steady stream, stirring with a wooden spoon. Cook, stirring constantly, for about 5 minutes until the mixture is thick and smooth.

Turn on to a wooden board or large plate, to form a circle 20cm (8in) in diameter and leave until cold and firm. Preheat grill (broiler) or heat a little oil in a frying pan (skillet). Cut coo-coo into wedges, brush on both sides with oil and grill (broil) or fry until browned. Serve with salsa.

Serves 6

VARIATIONS: Serve, without the salsa, with meat or fish dishes. It can be served immediately after cooking in the pan.

GLAZED SWEET POTATO

40g (1½oz/3 tablespoons) butter
3 tablespoons oil
1kg (2lb) sweet potatoes, cut into 1cm (½in) cubes
2 cloves garlic, crushed
2 pieces stem ginger, finely chopped
2 teaspoons ground allspice
2 teaspoons chopped fresh thyme
¼ teaspoon cayenne pepper
1 tablespoon syrup from the ginger jar
1 teaspoon brown sugar
salt
thyme sprigs, to garnish

In a frying pan (skillet), heat butter and oil. Add sweet potato cubes and fry, stirring frequently, for about 10 minutes until just soft. Stir in garlic, ginger and allspice. Cook, stirring, for 5 minutes.

Stir in thyme, cayenne pepper, ginger syrup, sugar and salt. Stir for 1-2 minutes until browned and tender. Serve garnished with thyme sprigs.

Serves 4

CHILLI CORNBREAD

115gm (4oz/1 cup) plain (all-purpose) flour
1 tablespoon baking powder
salt
½ teaspoon ground mace
115g (4oz/⅔ cup) cornmeal
2 eggs
300ml (10fl oz/1¼ cups) milk
50g (2oz/¼ cup) butter, melted
1 fresh red chilli, deseeded and very finely chopped
1 fresh green chilli, deseeded and very finely chopped
200g (7oz) can sweetcorn, drained

Preheat oven to 200C (400F/Gas 6). Grease and line a 900g (2lb) loaf tin (pan). Sift flour, baking powder, salt and mace into a large bowl. Stir in cornmeal. In a large jug, whisk together eggs, milk and melted butter. Make a well in centre of dry mixture and pour in liquid. Mix thoroughly until smooth.

Stir in red and green chillies and sweetcorn. Pour into prepared loaf tin (pan). Bake for 55-60 minutes until well risen, firm and lightly browned. Leave in tin (pan) for 5 minutes then turn on to a wire rack to cool.

Serves 8

BANANA BREAD

115g (4oz/½ cup) butter
115g (4oz/¾ cup) brown sugar
2 egg, beaten
225g (8oz/2 cups) plain (all-purpose) flour
1 tablespoon baking powder
1 teaspoon ground allspice
½ teaspoon grated nutmeg
3 ripe bananas, mashed
115g (4oz/¾ cup) chopped dates
115g (4oz/1 cup) roughly chopped pecan nuts
dried banana slices, to decorate

Preheat oven to 180C (350F/Gas 4). Grease
and line a 900g (2lb) loaf tin (pan). In a
bowl, beat together butter and sugar.
Gradually beat in egg. Sift flour, baking
powder, allspice and nutmeg into another
bowl. Stir sifted ingredients and the banana
alternately into egg mixture, beating after
each addition, until thoroughly blended.

Carefully stir in dates and pecan nuts.
Spoon mixture into prepared tin (pan).
Place dried bananas lightly on top. Bake for
about 1 hour until a skewer inserted into the
centre comes out clean. Leave in tin (pan)
for 5 minutes then turn on to a wire rack to
cool.

Serves 8

ORANGE SYRUP CAKE

5 oranges
115g (4oz/½ cup) softened butter
115g (4oz/½ cup) caster (superfine) sugar
2 eggs, beaten
175g (6oz/1 cup) semolina
100g (3½oz/scant 1 cup) ground almonds
1 teaspoon mixed spice
1½ teaspoons baking powder
ORANGE AND LIME SYRUP:
juice of 3 oranges
juice of 1 lime
115g (4oz/½ cup) caster (superfine) sugar
1 cinnamon stick, broken

Preheat oven to 180C (350F/Gas 4). Butter and base-line a 20cm (8in) round cake tin (pan). Grate rind from 1 orange and squeeze juice from one half. In a bowl, beat together butter, orange rind and sugar until light and creamy. Gradually beat in eggs. Mix together semolina, ground almonds, mixed spice and baking powder and fold into creamed mixture with reserved orange juice. Spoon mixture into the prepared tin (pan) and bake for 30-40 minutes until well risen and a skewer inserted into the centre comes out clean. Leave to cool in tin (pan) for a few minutes.

Meanwhile, peel and slice remaining oranges and set aside. To make syrup, in a pan, gently heat orange and lime juices, sugar and cinnamon. When sugar has dissolved, bring to boil and simmer for 30 minutes until syrupy. Turn cake on to a deep serving dish. Using a skewer, make holes in warm cake. Spoon or pour ¾ of the syrup over and leave for 30 minutes. Place reserved orange slices in remaining syrup and leave to cool. Serve with cake.

Serves 8

– CARIBBEAN CHRISTMAS CAKE –

700g (1½lb/4½ cups) luxury dried mixed fruit
225g (8oz/1¼ cups) ready-to-eat prunes, chopped
225g (8oz/1¼ cups) ready-to-eat dried mango,
  chopped
50g (2oz/⅓ cup) glacé (candied) cherries, quartered
700ml (25fl oz/3 cups) dark rum
225g (8oz/1 cup) butter, softened
250g (9oz/1⅓ cups) dark brown sugar
225g (8oz/2 cups) plain (all-purpose) flour
2 teaspoons baking powder
1 tablespoon mixed spice
6 eggs, beaten
4 tablespoons molasses
marzipan (almond paste) fruits or glacé (candied)
  fruits, to decorate

Put mixed fruit, prunes, mango, cherries and
600ml (20fl oz/2½ cups) rum in a saucepan.
Heat gently until beginning to boil, then
reduce heat and simmer for 5 minutes. Cool
then leave overnight. Preheat oven to 150C
(300F/Gas 2). Grease and line a 23cm (9in)
round tin (pan) and wrap a double layer of
brown paper round outside. In a bowl,
cream together butter and sugar until light
and fluffy. Sift flour, baking powder and
spice into a bowl, then gradually add flour
mixture to butter and sugar, alternating
with eggs, beating well after each addition.

Stir in molasses then stir into soaked fruits.
Spoon into prepared tin (pan) and smooth
the top. Bake for 2½-3 hours until a skewer
inserted into the centre comes out clean.
Prick cake all over with a fork and pour over
remaining rum. When sizzling stops, cool
cake in tin (pan). Remove from tin (pan)
and discard lining paper. Wrap in foil until
needed. To serve, decorate with marzipan
(almond paste) or glacé (candied) fruits.

Makes 23cm (9in) cake

——— JAMAICAN GINGER CAKE ———

225g (8oz/2 cups) self-raising flour
1 tablespoon ground ginger
¼ teaspoon freshly ground nutmeg
½ teaspoon bicarbonate of soda (baking soda)
115g (4oz/½ cup) butter
115g (4oz/¾ cup) dark brown sugar
2 eggs
1½ tablespoons golden (corn) syrup
1½ tablespoons milk
TOPPING:
6 pieces stem ginger, quartered
115g (4oz/1 cup) icing (confectioners') sugar
4 teaspoons syrup from ginger jar
lemon juice

Preheat oven to 170C (325F/Gas 3). Grease and line an 18cm (7in) square cake tin (pan). Sift flour, ginger, nutmeg and bicarbonate of soda (baking soda) into a bowl. Rub in butter then stir in sugar. Make a well in centre. In a bowl, whisk together eggs, syrup and milk. Pour into flour mixture and beat until smooth and glossy. Spoon into prepared tin (pan) and bake for 45-50 minutes until well risen and firm to the touch. Leave in tin (pan) for 30 minutes, then remove to a wire rack to cool completely.

To make topping, arrange ginger pieces on top of cake. Sift icing (confectioners') sugar into a bowl and stir in ginger syrup and enough lemon juice to make a smooth icing (frosting). Put icing (frosting) into a greaseproof paper (baking parchment) icing (piping) bag and drizzle over top of cake. Leave to set. Store in an airtight container for 1 day before cutting into squares and serving.

Makes 12 squares

—PINEAPPLE & COCONUT CAKE—

450g (1lb) can pineapple in natural juice, drained
150g (5oz/1¼ cups) plain (all-purpose) flour
115g (4oz/¾ cup) dark brown sugar
115g (4oz/½ cup) butter, softened
2 eggs
2 teaspoons baking powder
1 teaspoon ground allspice
50g (2oz/⅔ cup) desiccated (unsweetened flaked)
  coconut
TO DECORATE:
desiccated (unsweetened flaked) coconut
icing (confectioners') sugar

Preheat oven to 180C (350F/Gas 4). Cut
pineapple into large chunks. Grease and
base-line a 450g (1lb) loaf tin (pan). Place
flour and sugar in a food processor and blend
until thoroughly combined.

Add butter, eggs, baking powder, allspice and
coconut and process until smooth. Stir in
pineapple. Turn into prepared tin (pan).
Level surface and brush lightly with a little
cold water. Bake for 50 minutes until well
risen and a skewer inserted into centre comes
out clean. If it browns too quickly, cover after
40 minutes. Leave in tin (pan) for 10 minutes
then transfer to a wire rack to cool. Sprinkle
with desiccated (unsweetened flaked) coconut
and sift icing (confectioners') sugar on top.

Serves 8

JOURNEY CAKES

225g (8oz/2 cups) plain (all-purpose) flour
2 teaspoons baking powder
salt
1 teaspoon caster (superfine) sugar
25g (1oz/2 tablespoons) butter
oil, for frying

Sift flour, baking powder, salt and sugar into a large bowl.

Add butter and rub in until mixture resembles fine breadcrumbs. Alternatively, blend ingredients in a food processor. Add about 115ml (4fl oz/½ cup) cold water and mix to a stiffish dough. Divide into 8 pieces.

On an oiled board, flatten each piece slightly. Heat oil in a frying pan (skillet) and fry journey cakes, in batches, for 4-5 minutes on each side until golden brown. Drain on paper towels and serve hot with soup and stews.

Serves 4

NOTE: These little fried cakes are also known as Bakes or Johnny Cakes.

– CHEESE & CORNMEAL MUFFINS –

115g (4oz/1 cup) self-raising flour
1 tablespoon baking powder
¼ teaspoon cayenne pepper
salt
225g (8oz/2 cups) fine cornmeal
150g (5oz/1¼ cups) grated Cheddar cheese
50g (2oz/¼ cup) butter, melted
2 large eggs, beaten
300ml (10fl oz/1¼ cups) milk

Preheat oven to 200C (400F/Gas 6). Thoroughly grease 12 deep muffin tins (cups) or line cups with paper muffin cases. Sift flour, baking powder, cayenne pepper and salt into a bowl, then stir in cornmeal and 115g (4oz/1 cup) grated cheese. Pour melted butter into a bowl and stir in eggs and milk. Pour on to dry ingredients and mix quickly until just combined. Do not overmix.

Spoon batter into prepared muffin tins (cups). Scatter reserved cheese on top and bake for 20 minutes until golden brown. Leave to cool for a few minutes before transferring to a wire rack to cool.

Makes 12

— MANGO UPSIDE-DOWN CAKE —

225g (8oz/1 cup) butter
50g (2oz/⅓ cup) dark brown sugar
325g (11oz) can mango slices in syrup
175g (6oz/1 cup) light soft brown sugar
3 eggs, beaten
175g (6oz/1½ cups) self-raising flour, sifted
2 teaspoons ground ginger
1 teaspoon mixed spice

Preheat oven to 180C (350F/Gas 4). In a saucepan, melt 50g (2oz/¼ cup) butter. Stir in dark brown sugar. Spread over base of a 20-23cm (8-9in) cake tin (pan).

Drain mangoes, reserving 3 tablespoons syrup. Arrange mangoes in tin (pan). In a bowl, beat together remaining butter and the light brown sugar until light and fluffy. Gradually beat in eggs, adding 1 tablespoon flour towards the end. Fold in remaining flour, the ginger, mixed spice and reserved mango syrup.

Spread mixture over mango and bake for 55-60 minutes until sponge springs back when lightly pressed. Leave in tin (pan) for 5 minutes then turn on to a serving dish. Serve warm or cold.

Serves 6-8

—— COCONUT ICE CREAM ——

50g (2oz) creamed coconut
2 eggs, separated
115g (4oz/½ cup) caster (superfine) sugar
300ml (10fl oz/1¼ cups) single (light) cream
3 tablespoons coconut liqueur
150ml (5fl oz/⅔ cup) double (thick) cream, whipped
pulp of 6 passion fruit, to serve

Set freezer to maximum. In a bowl, blend
creamed coconut with 2 tablespoons hot
water. Add egg yolks and half the sugar and
beat well.

In a saucepan, heat single (light) cream.
Bring to the boil then pour on to egg yolk
mixture, stirring vigorously. Return to pan
and cook gently until slightly thickened.
Leave to cool. Stir in coconut liqueur. In
another bowl, whisk egg whites until stiff,
then whisk in remaining sugar. Fold into
whipped cream then fold in coconut
custard.

Pour mixture into a shallow freezerproof
container. Cover and freeze for 3 hours until
just frozen. Spoon into a bowl and mash
with a fork or whisk to break down ice
crystals. Return mixture to container and
freeze again for 2 hours, mash once more
then freeze for 2-3 hours until firm. Remove
from freezer and leave at room temperature
for 20-30 minutes before serving. Serve with
passion fruit pulp.

Serves 6

—BANANA & GINGER ICE CREAM—

450ml (16fl oz) can evaporated milk, chilled
115g (4oz/½ cup) light brown sugar
3 ripe bananas, mashed
2 tablespoons syrup from ginger jar
115g (4oz) preserved stem ginger, chopped
ginger syrup, to serve

Turn freezer to its coldest setting. Pour evaporated milk into a bowl and, using an electric beater, whisk until thick and mousse-like. Whisk in sugar.

Whisk bananas and ginger syrup into evaporated milk. Stir in chopped ginger. Cover and freeze for 3 hours until just frozen. Spoon into a bowl and mash with a fork or whisk to break down ice crystals.

Return mixture to container and freeze again for 2 hours. Mash once more then freeze for 2-3 hours until firm. Remove from freezer and leave at room temperature for 20-30 minutes before serving. Scoop into chilled glasses and serve with a little ginger syrup drizzled over.

Serves 6-8

— SPICED SWEET POTATO TART —

500g (1lb 2oz) sweet potatoes, diced
2 eggs, beaten
450ml (16fl oz/2 cups) evaporated milk
85g (3oz/⅓ cup) light brown sugar
1 tablespoon mixed spice
PASTRY:
175g (6oz/1½ cups) plain (all-purpose) flour
salt
85g (3oz/⅓ cup) butter
1 teaspoon caster (superfine) sugar
1 egg yolk

Cook sweet potatoes in boiling water for 10 minutes; drain thoroughly. Mash until smooth. Leave to cool. To make pastry, sift flour and salt into a bowl. Rub in butter to resemble breadcrumbs. Add sugar. Mix in egg yolk and enough cold water to make a firm dough. On a floured surface, roll out pastry and use to line a 23cm (9in) round flan tin (quiche pan). Chill for 30 minutes. Preheat oven to 190C (375F/Gas 5). Line pastry shell with greaseproof paper (baking parchment) and baking beans. Bake for 10 minutes. Remove paper and beans and return to oven for 5 minutes.

In a large bowl, mix together sweet potato, eggs, evaporated milk, sugar and mixed spice. Pour into pastry case (pie shell) and bake for 30 minutes. Reduce heat to 180C (350F/Gas 4) and bake for a further 10-15 minutes until filling is set. Serve hot or cold, dusted with icing (confectioners') sugar, if you like.

Serves 8

PINEAPPLE TART TATIN

300g (10oz) puff pastry
115g (4oz/½ cup) butter
115g (4oz/½ cup) granulated sugar
4 tablespoons double (heavy) cream
2 small-medium pineapples, total weight about 1kg
    (2lb), thinly sliced, cores removed

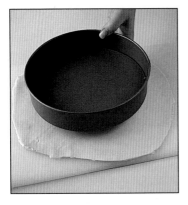

Preheat oven to 220C (425F/Gas 7). On a floured surface, roll out pastry to a circle slightly larger than a 22cm (8½in) non-stick sandwich tin (shallow cake pan). Transfer to a baking sheet, prick pastry lightly and chill.

In a small pan, gently heat butter and sugar until melted. Bring to the boil then simmer for 3-4 minutes, beating continuously until smooth, dark and fudge-like. Remove from heat, cool for 1 minute then beat in cream. If necessary, warm slightly then spoon into tin (pan). Arrange overlapping circles of pineapple slices in cake tin (pan).

Bake for 20-25 minutes until pastry is well risen and golden. Run a knife round the edge of pastry to loosen, then leave in tin (pan) for 2-3 minutes until juices stop bubbling. Invert on to a heatproof serving dish. Place under a hot grill (broiler) for 2-3 minutes to caramelize the top. Serve warm with crème fraîche sprinkled with a little nutmeg, if you like.

Serves 6

— FLAMBEED TROPICAL FRUIT —

1 small pineapple, peeled, cored and chopped
coarsely ground black pepper
1 teaspoon ground cinnamon
grated rind and juice of ½ orange
2 tablespoons light soft brown sugar
40g (1½oz/3 tablespoons) butter
1 large ripe mango, peeled and chopped
2 bananas, sliced
2 tablespoons rum

Put pineapple in a bowl. Season with pepper. Stir in cinnamon and orange rind. In a frying pan (skillet), heat sugar and butter until melted. Add pineapple and orange juice and cook for 3 minutes until beginning to soften.

Add mango and bananas to frying pan (skillet). Pour rum into a ladle or small pan, warm over a flame and ignite. Pour over fruit. When flames have died down, divide the fruit between four plates. Decorate with pineapple leaves, if you like.

Serves 4

—— BANANA & RUM BRULEE ——

200ml (7fl oz/scant 1 cup) coconut cream
400ml (14fl oz/1¾ cups) double (heavy) cream
1 vanilla pod, split
6 egg yolks
115g (4oz/½ cup) caster (superfine) sugar
2 small bananas, sliced
4 tablespoons dark rum
6 tablespoons brown sugar
mint leaves, to decorate

Preheat oven to 170C (325F/Gas 3). Put coconut cream, cream and vanilla pod in a saucepan and heat gently until almost boiling. Do not boil. In a bowl, whisk together egg yolks and caster (superfine) sugar until creamy. Strain in hot cream. Place bowl over a saucepan of simmering water. Stir continuously until custard is thick enough to coat the back of a spoon. In a bowl, toss together banana and rum. Divide among 6 ramekin dishes. Pour custard over.

Place dishes in a roasting tin (pan) and pour in hot water to come half-way up sides of ramekins. Bake for 5 minutes to create a skin on top. Allow to cool then refrigerate overnight. Preheat grill (broiler). Sprinkle brown sugar on top of custards and place under the hot grill (broiler) for 2-3 minutes until sugar melts and caramelizes. Leave for 3-4 hours to cool and set; decorate with mint leaves and serve with fresh fruit.

Serves 6

– GRILLED COCONUT PINEAPPLE –

4 tablespoons desiccated (unsweetened flaked)
  coconut
1 pineapple
2 tablespoons rum
50g (2oz/⅓ cup) brown sugar

Line a grill (broiler) pan with foil and
spread coconut over. Grill (broil) under a
low heat, stirring frequently, until just
toasted. Remove and set aside.

Using a sharp knife, cut pineapple, lengthwise, into 8 wedges, cutting right through
leaves and leaving them intact. Cut away
core. Sprinkle rum evenly over flesh.

Place pineapple wedges in grill (broiler) pan
and sprinkle brown sugar over. Grill (broil)
under a medium heat until sugar begins to
caramelize and pineapple is hot and
beginning to soften. Sprinkle over reserved
coconut.

Serves 4

CARIBBEAN CREPES

2 eggs
115ml (4fl oz/½ cup) coconut milk
175ml (6fl oz/¾ cup) milk
115g (4oz/1 cup) plain (all-purpose) flour
salt
1 tablespoon caster (superfine) sugar
15g (½oz/1 tablespoon) butter, melted
oil, for frying
sifted icing (confectioners') sugar, for dusting
FILLING:
40g (1½oz/3 tablespoons) butter
3 tablespoons light soft brown sugar
4 bananas, sliced
grated rind and juice of 1 orange
3 tablespoons dark rum

In a bowl, whisk together eggs, coconut milk and milk. Sift flour and salt into a mixing bowl. Stir in sugar. Make a well in centre of flour mixture and gradually beat in egg mixture to form a smooth batter. Stir in melted butter.

Heat a 20-23cm (8-9in) non-stick frying pan (skillet) and brush with a little oil. Pour in enough batter to coat base of pan, tipping pan so that the base is evenly coated. Cook crêpe until browned underneath and set on top. Turn over and cook other side. Remove from pan and keep warm while cooking remaining batter to make another 7 crêpes.

To make filling, melt butter in a heavy-based frying pan (skillet) and stir in sugar.

Add banana slices and cook, shaking pan frequently, for 1-2 minutes until beginning to soften. Add orange rind and juice and rum. Boil rapidly, until liquid is well reduced and slightly thickened.

Place a spoonful of banana filling on one quarter of each warm crêpe. Fold crêpes in half over the filling and then into quarters. Arrange 2 crêpes on each plate and dust with sifted icing (confectioners') sugar. Serve immediately.

Serves 4

—— SPICE ISLAND CRUMBLE ——

115g (4oz/½ cup) butter
4 firm bananas, cut into 2.5cm (1in) pieces
1 large ripe mango, peeled and cut into chunks
1 ripe papaya, peeled, deseeded and cut into chunks
4 ripe passion fruit
150g (5oz/⅔ cup) light brown sugar
juice of 1 orange
juice of 1 lime
150g (5oz/1¼ cups) plain (all-purpose) flour
1 teaspoon ground cinnamon
¼ teaspoon ground allspice
¼ teaspoon ground cloves
¼ teaspoon freshly grated nutmeg
115g (4oz/1⅓ cups) desiccated (unsweetened flaked) coconut
whipped double (heavy) cream and rum, to serve

Preheat oven to 190C (375F/Gas 5). Use 15g (½oz/1 tablespoon) butter to grease a large, shallow, ovenproof gratin dish. Arrange banana, mango and papaya pieces in dish. Cut passion fruits in half, scoop out the pulp and seeds and spread over fruit. Sprinkle with 3 tablespoons of the sugar, pour over orange and lime juices and gently mix fruit together.

Sift flour, cinnamon, allspice, cloves and nutmeg into a bowl. Stir in remaining sugar, and coconut. Rub in remaining butter until mixture resembles breadcrumbs. Sprinkle over fruit. Bake for 35-40 minutes until fruit is tender and top is brown and crisp. If topping browns too quickly, reduce heat. Stir a little rum into whipped cream and serve with crumble.

Serves 6

EXOTIC FRUIT SALAD

1 small watermelon
1 papaya, peeled, deseeded and chopped
3 mangosteens
1 small pineapple, peeled, cored and chopped
115g (4oz) blueberries
3 passion fruit
SYRUP:
150g (5oz/⅔ cup) caster (superfine) sugar
juice of 1 lime
rum, to taste (optional)
DECORATION:
strips of lime rind
mint leaves

To make syrup, place sugar and 150ml (5fl oz/⅔ cup) water in a saucepan. Heat gently until sugar has dissolved. Simmer for 5 minutes. Leave to cool. Add lime juice and rum, if using. Cut across watermelon to remove one third. Scoop out seeds and discard. Using a large melon baller, scoop out balls of flesh. Place in a bowl. Add papaya. Cut a zig-zag edge on larger melon shell.

Halve mangosteens, remove fruit and add to bowl with pineapple and blueberries. Halve passion fruit and scoop pulp and seeds into bowl of fruit and mix together. Transfer fruit to melon shell. Pour cooled syrup over. Decorate with strips of lime rind and mint leaves.

Serves 6-8

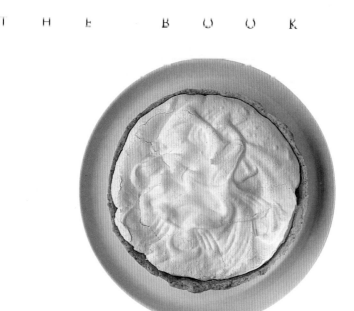

LIME & COCONUT MERINGUE PIE

25g (1oz/¼ cup) cornflour (cornstarch)
300ml (10fl oz/1¼ cups) coconut milk
grated rind and juice of 2 limes
2 large eggs, separated
175g (6oz/¾ cup) caster (superfine) sugar
PASTRY:
175g (6oz/1½ cups) plain (all-purpose) flour
salt
85g (3oz/⅓ cup) butter
1 teaspoon caster (superfine) sugar
1 egg yolk

To make pastry, sift flour and salt into a bowl. Rub in butter to resemble bread-crumbs. Add sugar. Mix in egg yolk, adding enough cold water to make a firm dough. On a floured surface, roll out pastry and use to line a 20cm (8in) loose-based flan tin (quiche pan). Chill for 30 minutes. Preheat oven to 190C (375F/Gas 5). Line pastry case with greaseproof paper (baking parchment) and baking beans. Bake for 15 minutes. Remove paper and beans and return pastry case to oven for 5-10 minutes until cooked. Turn oven down to 170C (325F/Gas 3).

In a saucepan, gradually combine cornflour (cornstarch) with coconut milk. Bring to a boil slowly, stirring constantly. Cook, stirring, for 3 minutes until thickened. Remove from heat and add the lime rind and juice, egg yolks and 50g (2oz/¼ cup) of the sugar. Pour into pastry case. Whisk egg whites until very stiff then gradually whisk in remaining sugar. Spread over filling and swirl with a palette knife. Bake for 10-15 minutes until lightly browned. Serve hot or cold.

Serves 6

QUEEN OF PUDDINGS

400ml (14fl oz) can coconut milk
25g (1oz/2 tablespoons) butter
grated rind of 1 lime
2 eggs, separated
50g (2oz/¼ cup) caster (superfine) sugar
85g (3oz/1½ cups) fresh white breadcrumbs
3-4 tablespoons guava jelly, warmed
shreds of lime rind, to decorate

Butter an 850ml (30fl oz/3¾ cup) oven dish.
Put coconut milk, butter and grated lime
rind in a saucepan and bring to the boil.
Remove from the heat. In a bowl, whisk
together egg yolks and half the sugar. Pour
in coconut milk mixture. Put breadcrumbs
in prepared dish and strain the coconut milk
mixture over. Leave to stand for 20 minutes
for breadcrumbs to swell. Preheat oven to
180C (350F/Gas 4). Bake the pudding for
30 minutes until lightly set. Remove from
oven.

Spread guava jelly over pudding. In a bowl,
whisk egg whites until stiff then whisk in
remaining sugar. Pile on top of pudding.
Bake for a further 10-15 minutes until
meringue is lightly browned. Scatter shreds
of lime rind over and serve.

Serves 4

– CARAMELIZED RICE PUDDINGS –

115g (4oz/⅔ cup) pudding (round-grain) rice
400ml (14fl oz) can evaporated milk
400ml (14fl oz/1¾ cup) milk
25g (1oz/2 tablespoons) caster (superfine) sugar
1 vanilla pod (bean), split lengthwise
1 cinnamon stick
grated rind of ½ orange
150ml (5fl oz/⅔ cup) double (heavy) cream
3 eggs
4 oranges
CARAMEL:
175g (6oz/¾ cup) caster (superfine) sugar
85ml (3fl oz/⅓ cup) water

To make caramel, put sugar and water into a small saucepan and heat gently until sugar dissolves.

Bring to the boil and boil gently, without stirring, until the liquid is golden. Remove pan from heat and allow to darken a little more. Divide caramel among 8 ramekin dishes and immediately carefully swirl dishes so that sides are well coated. Set dishes aside on a baking sheet.

Put rice, evaporated milk, milk and caster (superfine) sugar into saucepan. Add vanilla, cinnamon stick and grated orange rind. Gently bring to the boil, stirring. Cover, and simmer very gently, stirring occasionally, for 25 minutes until rice is tender.

Preheat oven to 170C (325F/Gas 3). Remove pan from the heat and allow rice to cool slightly. Remove vanilla and cinnamon.

In a bowl, whisk together cream and eggs then stir into rice. Spoon mixture over caramel in ramekin dishes. Bake for 30 minutes until firm.

Meanwhile, with a sharp knife, cut away all the skin and pith from oranges. Cut out segments by cutting down on either side of membrane. Reserve any juice and place in a bowl with the orange segments. Set aside. Carefully unmould rice puddings on to plates. Serve immediately with the orange segments and juice.

Serves 8

──────── RUM PUNCH ────────

225g (8oz/1 cup) granulated sugar
115ml (4fl oz/½ cup) fresh lime juice
350ml (12fl oz/1½ cups) golden rum
12 ice cubes
Angostura bitters
grated nutmeg
TO DECORATE:
fresh mint
slices of lime

Put granulated sugar and 225ml (8fl oz/ 1 cup) water in a saucepan. Bring slowly to the boil, stirring until sugar has dissolved.

Lower heat and simmer for 3 minutes. Remove from heat and set aside to cool. When completely cold, pour syrup into a jug.

Add lime juice, rum, ice cubes and 450ml (16fl oz/2 cups) water. Stir well then strain into glasses. Add a dash of Angostura bitters to each glass and sprinkle with nutmeg. Decorate with mint and lime slices and serve.

Serves 4

PINA COLADA

crushed ice
450ml (16fl oz/2 cups) fresh pineapple juice
225ml (8fl oz/1 cup) coconut milk
225ml (8fl oz/1 cup) white rum
DECORATION:
pineapple slices
cherries with stalks

Place crushed ice in 4 tall glasses to three-quarters fill.

Pour pineapple juice into a cocktail shaker or large screw-topped jar. Add coconut milk and white rum, and shake vigorously to blend. Pour into glasses over the ice.

To decorate, cut each pineapple slice into quarters and cut a slit half-way through each wedge. Place over rims of glasses. Hang cherries over glass rims and serve immediately.

Serves 4

—— TROPICAL PARTY PUNCH ——

400g (14oz) can mango slices
175g (6oz/¾ cup) granulated sugar
juice of 4 limes
juice of 4 lemons
150ml (5fl oz/⅔ cup) grenadine
250ml (9fl oz/generous 1 cup) white rum
1 litre (35fl oz/4½ cups) tropical fruit juice
1 litre (35fl oz/4½ cups) lemonade
ice cubes, to serve
TO DECORATE:
slices of orange
slices of lime

Empty mangoes and their syrup into a food processor and process to a purée.

Put granulated sugar and 175ml (6fl oz/ ¾ cup) water in a saucepan. Bring slowly to the boil, stirring, until sugar has dissolved. Lower heat and simmer for 3 minutes. Remove from heat and set aside to cool.

Add lime and lemon juice, mango purée, grenadine and rum. Stir well then chill. Just before serving, stir in tropical fruit juice and lemonade. Pour into 2 large jugs filled with ice cubes. Decorate with orange and lime slices.

Makes 16 glasses

— DRIVER'S PINEAPPLE PUNCH —

1 ripe pineapple
1 ripe mango
150ml (5fl oz/⅔ cup) traditional ginger beer
sparkling mineral water
juice of 1 lime

Cut top off pineapple and scoop out flesh, leaving shell intact. Discard core and reserve any juice.

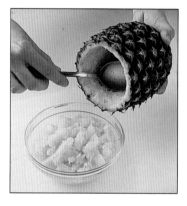

Peel mango and coarsely chop the flesh. Place pineapple pulp and juice to a blender or food processor. Add mango and ginger beer. Process until smooth.

Add sparkling water to thin to a drinking consistency and add lime juice. Pour punch into pineapple shell to serve.

Serves 2

INDEX